Sexual Assault in Context

Christopher Kilmartin
Alan D. Berkowitz

LEA LAWRENCE ERLBAUM ASSOCIATES, PUBLISHERS
Mahwah, New Jersey   London

Originally published 2001.

Lawrence Erlbaum Associates, Inc., Publishers
10 Industrial Avenue
Mahwah, New Jersey 07430

ISBN 0-8058-5542-4 paperback

Books published by Lawrence Erlbaum Associates are printed on
acid-free paper, and their bindings are chosen for strength and
durability.

Printed in the United States of America

Dedication

For my mother, Josephine Lily Kilmartin.

Contents

Deterrence and Empowerment Programs for Women • Summary and Conclusion

List of Figures

Acknowledgements

Thanks to all of my colleagues in sexual-assault programming and men's studies who have helped me to develop this approach over a number of years. I am especially grateful to Susan Bruce and Lisa Speidel, who took the time to review an initial draft of the manuscript and send me their reactions and suggestions. Mary Washington College supported this work with a faculty-development grant. In addition to generously allowing me to include his excellent work as Chapter 4, Alan Berkowitz also reviewed the manuscript prior to publication and is an outstanding colleague in the very important work of sexual-assault prevention. Thanks also to my life partner, Allyson Poska, who is a never-ending source of both intellectual stimulation and emotional support.

1
Providing a Gendered Context

There is no argument that males are the overwhelming majority of sexual-assault perpetrators. There are many possible explanations for this phenomenon, including men's socialization to be aggressive and to be sexual initiators, their disproportionate social and organizational power, and their ability to intimidate, based on greater size and muscle mass. Sexual assault is defined as unwelcome behavior, and therefore the potential perpetrator avoids committing the crime by making an accurate judgment about the potential victim's emotional reaction to the situation, and by caring whether or not he hurts another person. Masculine socialization and most male peer cultures discourage this kind of empathic, relationship-oriented activity.

Masculinity is one of the most powerful contexts within which sexual assault occurs, yet it is often left unaddressed in presentations on these topics. A gender-aware perspective entails an understanding of the social pressures on men to behave in culturally defined "masculine" ways, an awareness that they have choices about their behaviors, and an exploration of the consequences of their choices. Very few college men have such a perspective. Traditionally gendered men avoid learning about masculinity, as questioning the "macho ethic" may feel like one is unsure of oneself and therefore unmasculine. As a result, many men see sexual-assault programs as "male bashing" and/or as presentations on "women's issues" that do not concern them as long as they are not committing such behaviors.

Most colleges and universities provide programs on sexual assault for their students. The most basic level of programming involves defining the behaviors and their consequences for victims and perpetrators, as well as giving potential victims information about services available to them (e.g., self-defense courses, training in risk-reduction strategies, escort services, and resources available to survivors such as counseling, legal, and medical help). Most programs are successful at accomplishing these goals, however, all of these measures address only the behavior of victims/survivors and potential victims. If we are to move into the area of social change, we must address the behaviors and attitudes of potential perpetrators. Therefore, we must educate men about the psychological and social effects of the culture of masculinity — the social context that supports sexual assault. Males are pressured to avoid "feminine" behaviors, dominate women, take risks, be sexual conquerors, eschew any appearance of dependence, get the job done, and never take "no" for an answer. Although the antifeminine character of traditional masculinity (see Chapter 2) provides an atmosphere that condones and sometimes encourages the victimization of women, most men see sexual assaults as isolated events rather than as a reflection of a masculine culture in which they participate. And, because they can influence other men, they also have the potential for being an important part of prevention efforts.

If campus programming is to approach the goal of getting men involved in changing the destructive aspects of masculine culture, we must first help people understand how this culture is created and maintained. Men must learn to see themselves as gendered people if they are ever to understand women in similar context. Gender awareness allows men to question the often unarticulated assumptions under which they live and gives them the opportunity to choose the extent to which they will participate in the masculine cultural system. It also informs them of other negative consequences associated with hypermasculinity, such as physical risk, psychogenic disease, relationship problems, and substance abuse. This book is intended as an aid to people who are interested in initiating or improving men's campus programming by integrating masculine gender information into their discussions and exercises.

Limitations of "Behavior-Only" Programs

A feminist analysis of violence against women views rape and other partner violence as the worst symptom of a larger problem: a continuum of disrespect toward women. This continuum includes men's display of negative attitudes, e.g., through misogynist jokes, demeaning pornography, and infantalizing terms such as calling adult females "girls" and runs to the most extreme form of violence: gender-motivated murder. Such an analysis also emphasizes power imbalances between the sexes and the social forces that create and maintain these imbalances. Some programs for men do an excellent job of delivering this important context to the problem of gender-based violence. In other forms of sexual-assault educational programs, the focus is solely on telling men not to commit the crime of rape. These latter approaches ("behavior-only" programs) are limited in at least four critical ways:

- They communicate the expectation that merely refraining from sexual coercion is all that males need to do. Thus, they expect too little from men, who are capable of fully respectful relationships with women, and they may subtly encourage men to push to the legal limit of assaultive behavior.

- They fail to bring the positive message that men play a crucial role in reducing sexual assault, and they do not provide men with the knowledge or skills they need in order to do so.

- They contribute very little to men's self-awareness and overall psychological development.

- As attempts at persuasion, they fail to motivate men to change their behaviors or attitudes, and they may even push men in the opposite direction. Many men who attend these kinds of programs come away angry at what they perceive as "male bashing." They often remark, "I'm no rapist, so why do I have to listen to this?"

The Gender-Aware Approach

A gender-aware approach to sexual-assault prevention places the behavior of rape within the context of mainstream masculine cultural ideologies and customs. Men who participate in these kinds of educational programs will learn that:

- The culture of masculinity encourages men to think, feel, and behave in ways that are defined as "masculine."

- Two major influences attempt to enforce cultural masculinity. One is the childhood socialization of boys to behave in stereotypical ways by avoiding several behaviors: the display of vulnerable emotions, dependence on others, physical self-care, or any other indications of being feminine (as culturally defined, not as biologically ordained). The other is the set of social pressures of the moment that maintain socialization pressures, such as stereotypical media images and the threat of ridicule from male friends if one cries, challenges another man's disrespect of women, or expresses how much he loves his girlfriend.

- In every case, men have choices about how they respond to such pressure. Some men robotically conform to "macho" images of masculinity, others completely reject such standards for behavior, and most men's responses are somewhere between these two extremes. There is wide variation in men's levels of gender conformity, and most men overestimate the degree to which their peers fit traditional masculine stereotypes.

- The choices that men make in response to gender pressure have predictable consequences. Hypermasculine men are at risk for physical and mental-health problems, impoverished relationships, substance abuse, and violence perpetration, including sexual assault. Men who choose very low levels of conformity risk being ostracized or scapegoated by traditional men and may have to find alternative social support.

- Men are accountable for the choices that they make.

- Being able to understand gender pressure allows men to make more informed choices about their behavior rather than merely "going along with the program."

- Gender awareness can contribute positively to men's life goals in work, family, friendships, and leisure.

- Fully respectful relationships are the most comfortable and fulfilling ones for both men and women.

- Masculine peer culture can encourage negative behaviors such as sexual coercion. Men who participate in negative attitudes toward women contribute to sexual assault even if they never commit the crime. Sexual-assault prevention goes beyond merely refraining from the behavior and/or comforting assault survivors.

Men have powerful influences on male peers and can learn how to use their persuasive abilities in healthy ways. Men can participate in sexual-assault prevention by exerting these positive influences and they are responsible for doing so.

The gender-aware approach has the important characteristic of fitting with the central mission of higher education: the overall intellectual development of the person. When people understand how gender and other aspects of culture operate, they begin to think more critically about the world around them, to become better at evaluating evidence, to solve problems, and to grasp "the big picture" by putting information into context.

To illustrate, a "behavior-only," sexual-assault education program would define rape and consent. It would provide students with the rules under which they need to live in order to avoid violating the law and/or campus policy. It is of basic importance to furnish such information, but doing so provides little intellectual challenge to the student. It does not encourage the student to understand the cultural and historical context of the social problem being presented, or to reflect upon the impact of this problem on his or her life. It may even tell them how much negative behavior they can get away with before committing a crime and/or violation of campus policy.

In contrast, a gender-aware approach helps the student to understand the cultural significance of sexual assault, the personal and political effects of the problem, and the implications for participating in solutions. Thus, it not only encourages men to be responsible and respectful adults, it also contributes to their critical thinking skills. To illustrate with a parallel example, a debate in a speech class contributes to a student's overall intellectual development even if she or he never again deals with the content of the particular discussion. Whether or not the student ever again engages in any form of public debate, she or he is learning to obtain and evaluate evidence, understand the importance of the problem's social context, and take a reasoned position on the issue. Gender-aware dialogue on sexual assault helps a student to understand how problems have multiple facets, causes, and effects, even if that student never deals with sexual assault during his or her life. Moreover, when program professionals emphasize the positive aspects of relationships, students can apply what they learn to relationships of all kinds and are not limited to understanding the surface aspects of the phenomenon of victim and perpetrator.

Sexual-assault perpetrators are pathological individuals who make choices about their behavior and are responsible for those choices. At the same time, sexual assault is very rare or even nonexistent in many cultures. Anthropologists have discovered links between gender-based violence and a society's levels of aggressive masculine ideologies, physical/social separation of the sexes, and political/status differences between men and women (Coltrane 1998; Sanday 1981). Therefore, sexual assault is an individual problem within the context of powerful social influence. Men's social groups such as fraternities, athletic teams, or friendship groups can be microcosms of the kinds of cultural gender imbalances that set the stage for gender-based violence. These groups also have the potential to influence men in healthier directions.

Mainstream United States culture is perhaps the most highly individualistic culture in the history of the world. We tend to generate explanations for behavior that appeal solely to individual characteristics. For example, many people seem to believe that welfare recipients are lazy and/or exploitive of government systems, that people do not intervene in an emergency because they are callous, or that men are incapable of feeling and relationship orientation because they are men. Yet, considerable evidence indicates that situational and social influences wield a great deal of power in influencing behavior (see Asch 1965; Milgram 1963; Haney,

Banks, and Zimbardo 1973; Aronson 1999). In contrast to an individualistic belief system, a collectivist orientation views people as connected to each other as well as responsible for each other (Tavris and Wade 2000). Helping men to learn this alternative world view will not only allow them to participate in violence prevention, it will provide them a more sophisticated awareness of themselves and others.

A comprehensive, gender-aware approach to the education of men on college campuses can help to reduce the incidence of sexual assault by addressing the too-often ignored cultural support factor. It also has the important contribution of contributing to men's and women's overall relationship skills and health. Education researchers demonstrated long ago that teachers' and parents' low expectations have deleterious effects on students' academic performance (Rosenthal 1996). When we tell men that we merely expect them not to rape, we communicate very low expectations and very little empathy for the social pressures that men face. However, when we educate them about these pressures, are sensitive to the powerful influence of social forces, provide the knowledge and skills that they need in order to achieve fully respectful relationships, and communicate the expectation that we very much think that they are fully capable of being sensitive, skilled, and connected, we may be surprised at the level of their accomplishments.

Stages of Development in Men's Programming

Approaches to dealing with the problem of sexual assault develop and evolve over time. It is very difficult to put a highly effective program into place within a short period of time. In order to implement an effective program, professionals must:

- learn about the problem,

- undertake background research,
- conceptualize an approach,
- apply the approach to the characteristics of their campus population,
- secure the human and material resources necessary to implement their plan,
- respond to year-to-year changes in the campus climate, and
- evaluate the effectiveness of their programs.

Doing so requires a developmental approach. For example, in their early efforts, campus professionals might hire a guest speaker to give a public lecture on men and sexual assault or hire a consultant to train student personnel staff. The following year, they might integrate sexual-assault training for men into a staff member's job description and have that person deliver the information to fraternities and athletic teams. From there, the programming might grow to include a peer-education model, a public information campaign, and/or an academic course on men and masculinity.

Following is a stage model of men's programming development (note that this programming is in addition to other very important programming such as policy development/implementation/ enforcement, safety measures, and victim/survivor services). A campus task force or student-personnel unit may want to engage in long-term planning to develop the characteristics of advanced stages of the model.

Stage 1: No Male-Specific Programs

At this stage, nobody specifically addresses perpetrator issues or gender context in campus sexual-assault prevention efforts. Interventions are solely aimed at potential victims: campus lighting, escort services, risk reduction strategies, self-defense courses, and recovery services for survivors. All of these efforts are tremendously important, but a singular emphasis on victims/survivors absolves males from any responsibility for the problem, conceptualizes sexual assault as a "women's issue," and does not empower men to participate in solutions (Corcoran 1992).

Stage 2: "One-Shot" Programs for Interested Students

Often the first step in addressing men is to bring in a guest speaker or identify a faculty or staff member with expertise on the issue of sexual assault. The speech is sometimes part of a larger effort such as Women's History Month or a speakers' series, or it may be a reaction to a critical incident, such as a highly-publicized assault. If the speaker is skillful and delivers good information, this approach begins to break men's silence about the problem of sexual assault, identifies the problem as a men's issue, and stimulates campus dialogue around programming for men. If attendance is voluntary, only the most interested students, i.e., the ones who seem to need to hear the message least, are likely to participate, which presents both a problem and an opportunity. On the one hand, there is no information delivered to the general student population, except perhaps in media coverage of the event. On the other hand, the presentation may allow staff to identify and increase the commitment of the most interested students, who may be willing to help develop further efforts. The most frequent limitation of this kind of program is that students forget about the issue shortly after the event unless someone plans and executes some sort of follow-up. And, most experts on the topic are significantly older than most students, which often limits their influence compared with that of an age peer.

Stage 3: Mandatory Participation in Brief Programming

At this level, male students are required to attend a "one-shot" program on sexual assault. These programs are often mandatory for intercollegiate athletes, fraternity pledges, or all first-year students as part of orientation and/or a first-year experience program. The length of these presentations varies from 20 minutes to two hours or more, and formats vary from lectures to small group discussions to theatrical presentations. The obvious advantage of this approach is that it addresses all of the male population in the group, an especially important component with at-risk men. (Fraternity men and athletes show disproportionately high levels of perpetration, although one must be careful not to stereotype individual fraternities or teams. See Boswell and Spade 1996, for a discussion of the characteristics of high-risk and low-risk fraternities). It is recommended that these kinds of programs be carried out in all-male groups with a male presenter (see Chapter 3). As with Stage 2 approaches, the influence of non-age peers and the fleeting nature of the intervention limits the effectiveness of these kinds of programs. However, mandatory participation often signifies that some factions of the campus community have identified sexual assault as a significant problem worthy of addressing, and this is a good early step toward more extensive efforts at prevention.

Stage 4: More Extensive Programming with Mandatory or Voluntary Participation

At this stage, male students attend a series of events in which they learn more about men's role in preventing sexual assault. In one such model program, selected fraternity men participate in a full semester seminar on violence against women, for which they earn academic credit (Mahlstedt 1998, see Chapter 3 on the Fraternity Violence Education Project). The clear advantage of this approach is that it keeps the issue in front of the men. Their under-standing and reactions to the problem will evolve, and thus there is an opportunity to process the development of their thoughts and feelings about sexual assault and related issues such as sexism, ho-mophobia, the culture of violence, and power relationships between the sexes.

Stage 5: Peer Education and Public-Awareness Campaigns

Well-trained and talented peer educators are a very powerful resource for campus rape prevention. They have a credibility that no staff member can attain, a participative awareness of campus culture, and a great many day-to-day interactions with the target audience. It takes considerable resources to identify and train peer educators who can be effective presenters, and therefore the staff person in charge must be able to put considerable time and effort into developing and implementing such a program. But the reward of doing so successfully is a high level of sexual-assault prevention effectiveness. Public awareness efforts such as The White Ribbon Campaign and the Social Norms Approach (see Chapter 3) move the dialogue of men's violence against women into the mainstream of campus life. These kinds of undertakings can be an important outreach component of peer education.

Stage 6: Fully Integrated Programming

This level involves a coordinated effort to fully address the problem of sexual assault on campus in a way that contributes to students' overall intellectual, moral, and personal development. It involves highly effective policies, frequent awareness campaigns, peer education, assault-prevention training for all members of the community, well-developed academic coursework on gender, outreach, and social change efforts, and a commitment to gender equity in the campus power structure and community values.

Goals of Gender Aware Programming for Men

☑ To educate men about the effect of gender on their lives.

☑ To invite men to explore gendered issues:

- fear ("femiphobia") or hostility (misogyny) toward women
- homophobia
- anger and other feelings
- sexuality
- feelings about their fathers and other men
- relationships
- the pressures of cultural standards of masculinity

☑ To facilitate empathy for women, other men, and the self.

☑ To associate masculinity with dignity and individual choice.

☑ To define and denormalize sexual assault and the underlying negative attitudes toward women.

☑ To identify the characteristics of healthy relationships and learn the skills need to develop these kinds of relationships.

☑ To learn how to positively affect other men.

☑ To contribute to men's overall intellectual, moral, and psychological development.

2
The Content

Sexual assault takes place within the context of a culture that encourages males to experience themselves and to behave in certain ways. Embedded within these cultural messages are attitudes toward the self, women, sexuality, and power. A full understanding of coercive sexuality must include an awareness of the cultural gender context in which these behaviors take place. This chapter is a description of the content of male gender-role education programs. Presenters should have a solid background in gender theory and research, and they should use their personalities and creativity to present the information in an engaging way. Additional resources can be found in Appendix A. An outline of the text material in this chapter is in Appendix B. The following is written as if the author is talking to an audience of college men. Presenters should adapt this material to suit their styles and the characteristics of their programs.

Gender Information for Men

College is obviously a time when people are preparing for their futures in a variety of ways. Your general education and across-the-curriculum requirements are designed to improve your basic skills in critical thinking, written and spoken expression, and general knowledge. Your major program gives you the background you will need to enter the working world, and your career office provides you with resources you can use in the quest to find a rewarding career that makes good use of your talents, values, and interests.

Many aspects of your life after college will involve dealing with other people, whether it is as friends, co-workers, subordinates, supervisors, spouses, life partners, children, or in some other relationship. Although college is clearly a time when people are learning about relationships, there are not too many places in the college experience where you have the opportunity for specific education in this area. This is especially true for men, who are not encouraged to think of themselves in relationship terms. This program/presentation is an attempt to provide this education.

Because relationship orientation is considered a feminine quality, many men avoid talking about relationships, despite the fact that the vast majority of men are interested in having quality relationships, which are, for many people, one of the most important aspects of living. Females are often encouraged to see themselves within the context of relationships from the earliest age. For example, parents and friends often give little girls dolls, and playing with dolls is a kind of rehearsal for being in a relationship with someone. When boys get dolls, it is usually G. I. Joe, which is not about relationships; it is about doing some task. It doesn't matter how a boy *feels* about G. I. Joe or what he thinks G. I. Joe feels about himself or the boy. The world of relationships has a great deal to do with the world of gender. Therefore, if we are to teach people about relationships, we have to teach them about gender at the same time.

Gender and How it Operates

Gender is a set of cultural forces that pressure people to experience themselves and to behave in certain ways based on whether they are male or female. Beginning very early in life, we get messages telling us that the emotional, relationship, and working lives of males and females are supposed to be different in many ways. These messages are reinforced by media, institutional practice, friends, and acquaintances. Some examples:

Media: In many television programs and movies, men are often portrayed as incompetent in relationships, housekeeping, and other "feminine" activities. Women are rarely portrayed as physically competent and are often portrayed as attracted to men who fit the cultural stereotype of violence, risk taking, dominance, and emotional disconnection. Beer commercials in which actors are used nearly always involve men playing sports, working, or doing outdoor things, and they often involve women as sexually provocative.

Institutional practice: There are large discrepancies in the proportions of women and men who become police officers, nurses, elementary school teachers, engineers, stockbrokers, etc. Overtly or subtly, many people are steered into gender-stereotypical occupations by a number of forces. Gay and lesbian people are currently not allowed to marry. Marriage is a cultural institution set up to legally define the relationship of one man and one woman, and it historically has taken the form of the woman becoming the man's property. Think about the language — "Who gives this woman to be married to this man?" and "You may now kiss the bride." (as if the woman were only the passive recipient of the kiss and does not participate in it).

Friends and acquaintances: People who behave in non-stereotypic ways may not be accepted by others. For example, what would happen if a man talked with his male friend in the following way? "Mike, I've been *so* upset since we had that argument. I could hardly sleep last night. Are you *sure* you're really not mad at me?" (Brannon 1985, p. 307). A man who behaves aggressively may be considered "forceful" but the same behavior in a woman might result in her being called a "bitch."

Beliefs about Sex Differences

Despite the fact that people tend to think of males and females as different, research indicates that the sexes are overwhelmingly more similar than different. The diversity within women as a group and within men as a group is greater by far than the small differences we see between the *average* behaviors of males and females. The average man is taller than the average woman, but a very tall woman is taller than most men, and a very short man is shorter than most women. The average man is more physically aggressive than the average woman, but most men are not violent, and some women are.

If we were to graph a population on some characteristic, we would nearly always produce a normal curve, with a few people on each extreme and most people clustered around the middle. For example, if we were to measure many people's intelligence, a few ould be on the extreme right side of the curve (we would call these people intellectually gifted), a few would be on the extreme left (we would call these people developmentally delayed or retarded) and the vast majority of people would cluster around the middle.

Figure 1. The Normal Curve

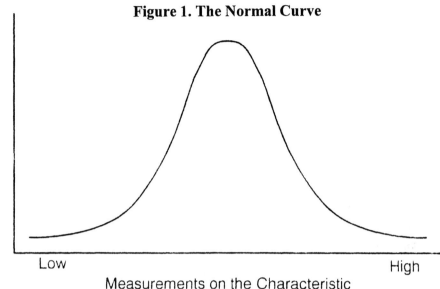

Most people assume that if we were to graph separate populations of men and women on characteristics such as violence, emotional expression, mathematical ability, verbal ability, mechanical aptitude, etc., it would look like Figure 2.

Figure 2. A Large Sex Discrepancy

However, this is not the case. In most areas, there are no aver-age differences between the sexes. In the areas in which we do find average differences, they look like Figure 3.

Figure 3. A Small Sex Discrepancy

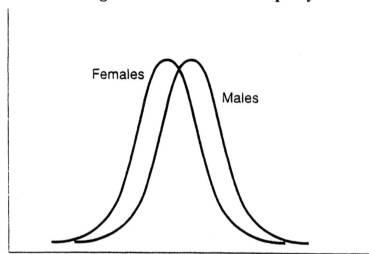

Research indicates that average sex differences rarely account for more than 5-10 percent of the variance in people's behavior. But people still talk about the "opposite sex" and the "battle of the sexes" despite the facts that the sexes are not opposite at all (repro-ductive roles are complementary, not opposite) and the overwhelm-ing majority of "combatants" in the "battle" are allegedly in love with and having children with the "enemy." The only four behav-iors in which we see large differences between men and women are the reproductive ones: lactation, impregnation, gestation, and men-struation. (Note to presenters: for a discussion of the available re-search on sex comparison, see Kilmartin 2000; Hyde and Plant 1995).

Speaking of men and women as opposites is like describing an Apple computer as the opposite of an IBM computer. Language is powerful, and this kind of mentality affects what we expect in relationships and interactions. If we think of men and women as opposites, then we do not expect to have anything in common with the other sex, and therefore we may be less likely to seek them out for friendships or other kinds of relationships (except for sexual ones, if we are heterosexual). If we behave in such a way, we create a vicious cycle whereby we expect other-sex people to be different; therefore we avoid them; therefore we never learn what we have in common with them; therefore we expect them to be different.

Gender roles may have a small component of biological influence, but they are mainly learned. Cross-cultural and historical variation in gender patterns tells us that culture creates many possibilities for gender arrangements. For example, many Italian men are emotionally expressive, most Russian dentists are women, there is a greater proportion of female athletes in the United States than there was 50 years ago while the proportion of male athletes has remained about the same relative to the population, urban areas have more flexible gender roles than rural ones, and industrialized societies have more flexible gender roles than agricultural societies.

Effects of Gender Pressure

Gender is a set of social pressures to behave in certain ways, however, the responses of *individual* men and women to these pressures are highly variable — we all know very emotional men or very ambitious women, men who don't like sports or women who do. In fact, *most* people feel that they do not fit the cultural stereotype for their sex. Moreover, gender has unconscious and emotional components. People are not always aware of the effects of gender on their lives.

Gender pressures operate somewhat like the default options on a computer. Your computer has features that are set at the factory and will not change unless you change them. For example, the size of the icons on your initial screen is a default option. Three conditions are necessary to change it. First, you must know that it is an option and thus possible to change. Second, you must be motivated to change the option. Perhaps you know it's an option but are satisfied with the size of the icons, and therefore you would be unlikely to change it. On the other hand, perhaps your eyesight is poor and so you want them to be bigger, or perhaps you want to fit a lot of icons on the screen, and so you need them to be smaller. Third, you have to know *how* to change them, to execute the right sequence of operations to put the alternative option into effect.

Although gendered behaviors are not "set" at the "factory" nor are they as simple as computer features, the parallel is that they are so much a part of our everyday lives that it is easy to go along with them if we don't think about it. And like computer features, we might want to "customize" our gender behaviors to fit our particular needs. But it is sometimes said that, "the fish is never aware of the water." Gender is so much a part of the culture that it is often invisible to us, making it difficult to make informed choices about options, as we are often unaware that these options even exist.

This program/presentation is about making informed choices about gendered behavior rather than merely conforming to stereotypes. It is about giving you the language to understand what the default options are and putting you into the position to make *informed* choices based on your individual values, beliefs, and characteristics. Within every group of people will be a wide variation of responses to gender pressure. Some people conform very strongly to gender role stereotypes; some reject these images completely; most people fall somewhere in between.

Most people behave more gender stereotypically in public than in private, indicating that a significant component of gendered behavior is in the fulfillment of a social role rather than merely the expression of ingrained characteristics. For example, a man may attend a sad movie and feel like crying, but he may stifle this expression because he would be embarrassed to be thought unmasculine. If people looked at this man and thought him to be unemotional, they would be incorrect, confusing a public appearance with an internal characteristic. We can go back to the earlier example, in which one man says to another, "Mike, I've been *so* upset since we had that argument. I could hardly sleep last night. Are you *sure* you're really not mad at me?" It is quite possible that this man *feels* this way but doesn't *talk* this way, and so it's important to keep in mind that a person's social behavior doesn't always exactly correspond with who that person is on the inside. You may behave in very different ways with your friends than with your parents, which may both be different from the way you behave in the presence of your professors. We often alter our behavior to fit our relationships and social roles.

Regardless of this social pressure to conform to gender stereotypes, in every case people have choices about the extent to which they "go along with the program," and they are responsible for the choices they make. For example, if a man gets into an argument with another man, sometimes he feels that he should "settle the disagreement" by engaging in a physical fight to defend the "honor" of his masculinity. If he does so, he is subject to arrest for assault, he risks his physical health, and if he hurts the other man, he has to deal with the emotional and other implications of having done so.

If this man had different ideas about what is important in masculinity, he probably would perceive the other man differently as well as behave differently. Gender ideologies affect what we expect of people, what we notice about them, what we remember about them, and how we interact with them. Mainstream U.S. cultural stereotyping often puts gender into places where it does not belong, such as in color preferences, personality, types of drinks, how one should sit, how one should carry books, etc. For example, we sometimes think of the color pink as being for women, when any man is just as likely as any woman to look good (or not so good) in that color. In bars, men are expected to order a drink that is brown, like beer or whiskey, and avoid a colorful drink such as a Screwdriver or a Cape Cod. These cultural arrangements are arbitrary — a man is just as likely as a woman to enjoy a Screwdriver or a Cape Cod.

Origins of Gender Roles

Historically, gender roles seem to be constructed around the work that a society needs to do. When upper body strength and reproduction were important, societies developed gender roles that reflected men's and women's physical characteristics, and ideologies about men's and women's "nature" followed. For example, when some members of a society have to risk their lives for others (such as in war or dangerous hunting), those tasks have usually gone to men for at least three reasons. First, men have greater upper body strength and thus they were more suited to those kinds of tasks before people developed machinery. Second, men's necessary role in the reproductive process (a few seconds) is much briefer than women's (nine months plus), and therefore men can range farther from the home without disrupting the society's need to produce more children. Third, because one man can impregnate many women, the loss of men has little effect on the group's ability to produce children.

There is some cultural variation to standards of masculinity within the United States and the world, but there is a great deal of overlap in masculine ideologies among different cultural groups, reflecting many cultures' historically common societal needs for defense, reproduction, and social arrangements. Some cultures are completely different — in Tahiti, there are very few social arrangements that differentiate between men and women. Anthropologists believe that Tahiti is different because there is plenty of food, no dangerous hunting, and it is a remote island that has never been attacked. There is no need in Tahiti to make men into warriors or to differentiate the kinds of work that men and women do (see Gilmore 1990).

Gender roles in the United States and elsewhere in the world are changing in response to changes in the character of work, which evolves in response to new types of economies, labor saving devices, and reproductive technologies and needs. In the case of war in industrialized society, technology makes it equally likely that a woman could be as skilled a fighter pilot as a man. Because of improved food production techniques and machinery, hunting is no longer really necessary. And because of overpopulation and the needs of industrial and information age societies, most people cannot afford and/or choose not to have as many children as their parents and grandparents had. We also have reproductive technologies that were previously unavailable. Thus, women's young adult lives are less likely than in previous generations to be devoted to multiple pregnancies and births.

Gender roles will continue to evolve in the future. Increasingly, men and women will be equally capable of doing most kinds of both work and family tasks, as we are beginning to see with phenomena such as telecommuting and "house husbands." Holding on to 1950s ideas of the social places of men and women will become increasingly untenable as gender roles become more and more flexible. People's individual styles, occupations, and the needs of their primary relationships will dictate their behavior much more than socially prescribed roles for men and women, allowing people to

maximize their potentials without having opportunities limited by
social prejudices based on their hormones, genitalia, and chromo-
somes.

Gender Pressures and Men

Cultural masculinity is a set of gender pressures placed on
males. Central to the masculine gender role is *antifemininity* —
men are expected to avoid culturally defined feminine behaviors at
all costs. These include wearing pastel colors, being emotionally
expressive, talking with other men about how much we love our
girlfriends, and asking for directions when we are lost in the car.
Remember that men's responses to these pressures vary widely.
Men can perform any of these behaviors if they think that doing so
is important enough to resist the cultural pressure to behave otherwise.

The antifeminine nature of masculinity means that men are
expected to constantly prove a negative, which is impossible. Men
who conform to masculine ideologies refuse to back down from a
fight not because they want to dominate or be violent. Rather, they
do so in order to avoid being considered weak or worrying about
getting hurt, which are defined as feminine. But you can never
prove what you are not. Winning, risk taking, and controlling your
emotions today does not mean that you will be able to do these
things tomorrow, and so many hypermasculine men compulsively
try to prove the unprovable over and over again. For example,
when the San Francisco 49ers won their second straight Super
Bowl, some of the players were talking about winning again next
year before the game had even ended!

Men who accept masculine ideologies try to avoid a long list
of culturally defined feminine behaviors and experiences, such as:

- vulnerable emotions (most feelings except for anger and
  lust),

- dependence on others,
- relationship orientation,
- concern for their physical safety,
- doing what they believe to be "women's work," such as child care,
- asking for help,
- getting emotionally close to other men,
- exhibiting feminine mannerisms like carrying books at the chest instead of on one's side, and
- engaging in feminine activities like shopping or calling a friend "just to chat."

The "rules" of masculinity (Brannon 1985) are:

- "No sissy stuff" — avoid feminine behaviors.
- "Be a big wheel" — strive for status and achievement, especially in sports and work.
- "Be a male machine" — solve problems without help, maintain emotional self-control at all times, and never show weakness to anybody.
- "Give 'em hell" — take physical risks and be violent if necessary.

Remember that no man is required to follow these "rules." He can resist the cultural pressure if he believes that it is important to do so.

Antifemininity is used to enforce conformity to masculine behavior norms. Males can be socially ostracized or even attacked if they behave in feminine ways. One of the worst insults that one can level at a boy is that he throws, runs, talks, or acts like a girl. Antifemininity encourages men to see themselves as having nothing in common with women. It also encourages men to view feminine traits and females as less valuable than masculine traits and males. Therefore, antifemininity feeds the disrespect of women and inhibits the formation of men's friendships with women as well as equal-partner types of romantic relationships with them. However, many men are able to achieve these kinds of relationships with women by resisting the cultural pressure of the antifemininity norm.

Antifemininity also inhibits men from learning from women. Many culturally defined feminine traits and skills (e.g., emotional expression, relationship sensitivity, self-protection) have important implications for people's quality of life, yet many men avoid taking on these traits and learning these skills because they fear being considered unmasculine. Again, many are able to resist the pressure to be hypermasculine and take on these useful feminine characteristics.

One of the most feminine kinds of behavior is getting too emotionally close to other men. Masculinity tends to sexualize all intimacy even though intimacy can be nonsexual and sexuality can be nonintimate. *Homophobia*, the fear of same sex attraction, is related to antifemininity and is also used to enforce gender conformity in men. Another worst insult to level at a male is to suggest that he is sexually attracted to other males. Homophobia can reduce men's friendships to "male bonding" — an exclusive focus on sports, work, women, cars, stereos, and other stereotypically masculine topics — that keeps men at an emotional arm's length from each other. Many men are dissatisfied with the fact that they have a lot of "buddies" (men they do things with) but very few friends (people who know them well and support them emotionally).

Advantages and Disadvantages
of Conforming to Gender

Conformity to masculine ideologies has several advantages. Men who accept hypermasculine ideologies have a fairly clear "roadmap" for behavior and a convenient "yardstick" for measuring their worth. They feel good if they can live up to masculine standards of behavior and experience by making a lot of money, appearing self-assured, doing well athletically, and having sex with many different women. If they are successful, they can garner the approval and admiration of others in many situations and attain a sense of power. Because of the cultural valuing of masculinity, there is a high likelihood that others will take them seriously. The masculine orientation of achievement, problem solving, and hard work contributes to the greater good. Hypermasculine men also report an infrequent and/or less intense experience of negative emotions than others.

Conforming to cultural standards of masculinity also has disadvantages. Men who accept hypermasculine ideologies feel that they must always compete and achieve, as they are compulsively trying to prove a negative — that they are not feminine — which is impossible. Although their relative lack of negative emotions may make them more comfortable than others at times, it is accompanied by a less frequent and/or less intense experience of positive emotions.

Perhaps the most serious disadvantage of hypermasculinity is in its negative effects on men's physical health. Men die an average of seven years earlier than women. They commit suicide four times more often, are at greater risk for most serious diseases, are injured more often, are more likely to use tobacco, drink to excess, refuse to see a doctor or wear seat belts, and engage in a number of other health risks.

There also are characteristically masculine mental-health problems. Men abuse alcohol and other drugs more frequently, are hospitalized in psychiatric facilities following a relationship breakup much more frequently than women, and, because they are unlikely to reveal themselves or have intimate relationships, hyper-masculine men receive little social support from others when they are emotionally needy. As a result, they often suffer from loneliness.

Violence is unmistakably masculine in mainstream U.S. culture. Males commit over 90 percent of violent crimes, and there are currently more than one million men in federal prisons. Injuries that men inflict on their female partners are the most likely cause for women's emergency room treatment for the 15- to 44-year-old age group, and sexual assault of women by men is a very serious problem. Not surprisingly, nearly all violence by men is linked to the acceptance of hypermasculine ideologies, such as the beliefs that violence is an acceptable way to solve problems, that "real men" never back down from a fight, and that they should control women at all costs.

(Note to presenters, for references to the above, see Kilmartin 2000 and other references listed in Appendix A.)

Social advantages and disadvantages are gender-based to an extent. To be male in U.S. culture is to have a set of social advantages, such as the freedom to express one's sexual needs, occupational opportunity, and lower fear of gender-based violence relative to women. It is important to understand that these advantages do not apply to all men in equal shares. Wealthy, white, attractive, heterosexual, able-bodied, and athletic men tend to reap more advantages than other men.

At the same time, there are social "disadvantages to the advantages" of being male, such as paying full price for drinks at "ladies nights," having one's value as a person based on one's athletic and business accomplishments, and having others pay little attention to our physical or emotional pain.

To be female in U.S. culture is to have a set of social disadvantages, such as lower pay than males for the same work, having one's value as a person based on one's attractiveness, and disproportionate exposure to sexual harassment, sexual assault, and other forms of gender-based violence. As with men's advantages, women's disadvantages do not apply to all women in equal shares. Wealthy, white, attractive, heterosexual, and able-bodied women tend to reap fewer disadvantages than other women.

There are social "advantages to the disadvantages" of being female, such as paying less than full price for drinks at "ladies nights," getting a good deal of attention if one is attractive, and sometimes having others pay attention to one's physical or emotional pain (Berkowitz 1999).

Gender-based social advantages and disadvantages are best viewed in relative terms and multiple contexts. One cannot consider a person privileged merely because that person enjoys some isolated advantage. For example, a "big picture" analysis would never consider the following people privileged: handicapped people because they get good parking places, people in prison because they don't have to pay for their meals, or people in menial jobs because they don't have to take their work home with them.

Likewise, one cannot consider a person underprivileged merely because that person suffers some isolated disadvantage. For example, a "big picture" analysis would never consider the following people to be underprivileged: people who can afford to hire maids and servants because it compromises their privacy, famous people because their fans want to talk with them when they go out in public, or strikingly attractive people because they get so much attention from people who want to date them.

The Future of Gender

As we look to the future of gender relations, we see that traditional masculinity and traditional femininity are becoming outmoded for a number of reasons, some of which I have already mentioned. First, reproductive technologies and overpopulation mean that couples can decide when and if they will have children, and they can decide how many they will have. Except for breastfeeding, men can perform every parenting behavior. Therefore, reproductive roles are much more flexible than ever. Second, upper body strength is no longer an important economic asset, as labor saving devices are now available for most tasks. There is no good reason for there to be a division of labor based on "women's work" and "men's work." Third, we are moving from an industrial to an information-based economy, and therefore people can even work at home.

Because of these changes, women are becoming equal economic partners. Therefore "breadwinning" no longer exclusively defines masculinity and homemaking no longer exclusively defines femininity. Heterosexual couples have a greater amount of options in negotiating their work and family roles.

Masculinity and Life Goals

Men who want to prepare themselves for maximum opportunity, functioning, health, and fulfillment would do well to undertake an examination of the gendered forces that influence their lives and make affirmative choices about their behavior based on their values and goals. Most college men want to have a successful college career and graduate. They want to enter the working world, do well, and be financially successful. They see themselves in leadership positions in their careers. Nearly all men will be working with women, with perhaps the exception of off-shore oil workers and other unusual occupations. Many will have female supervisors at some points during their working lives. Since they will spend much of their lives at work, men want to have good relationships with their co-workers, subordinates, and supervisors. Most heterosexual men want to someday marry, have children, and have satisfying family relationships.

Gender awareness will serve men in all of these goals. Some men fear that they will have to give up the enjoyable and adaptive aspects of traditional masculinity in order to deal with a changing gender world, but it is not an "either/or" proposition. Rather than tearing down traditional masculinity, men can expand their notions of masculinity in the following ways:

- Independence is masculine. Men can be independent by refusing to conform to stereotypical gender demands when they think it is important to do so.

- Facing a challenge is masculine. Men can face challenges by learning skills that are adaptive but that also have been defined as feminine, such as dealing with vulnerable emotions, gaining relationship skills, expanding their interests beyond work and sports, and learning how to confront male peers who behave in sexist and/or self-destructive ways.

- Leadership is masculine. Men can be leaders by showing other people a healthier and more modern vision of masculinity.

- Risk taking is masculine. Men can take reasonable emotional risks by revealing themselves to others in the service of building relationships.

- Courage is masculine. It takes a good deal of courage to negotiate one's life without using the stereotypical roadmap of masculinity. It takes great courage to challenge other men who behave in offensive or unhealthy ways.

- Assertiveness is masculine. Men can be assertive by exercising their rights to express their feelings, questioning outmoded notions of masculinity, and asking for what they want in relationships.

Many men have distorted notions of the meaning of masculine attributes, and we would do well to undertake an exploration of these values. *Courage* is facing risk because a successful outcome is important to one's principles and goals. Many men narrowly define risk as only physical or financial, but risk can be emotional or relationship-oriented. *Bravado* is pretended courage — facing risk in order to avoid being evaluated as weak, such as when a man engages in a fight with a bigger opponent because he does not want to be considered unmasculine. It is thus courageous to say to male friends, "I don't like the way you talk about women. I think you should have more respect for them." Or "I feel very badly since my girlfriend broke up with me. I need your help." Or "I like you; I'm glad you're my friend."

Loyalty is being faithful to others to whom one has made a commitment. With male friends, many men confuse loyalty with the notion that "anything my friend does is all right with me." It is very disloyal to witness a friend doing something destructive to himself or others and not challenge him. It is disloyal to one's female friends, relatives, and partner to condone or encourage male friends' sexist behaviors and attitudes.

Independence is freedom of action. It means that one makes up one's own mind about behavior and attitudes rather than blindly conforming to others' opinions. *Counterdependence* or *oppositionalism* is behaving in contrary ways merely to avoid the appearance of being dominated by another person, such as when a man treats his female partner badly in the company of his male friends in order to gain their approval. Although men think of themselves as independent, there is tremendous conformity to masculine ideologies, behaviors, and attitudes in all-male social groups.

Respect is courteous regard, attention, and consideration for others' feelings and experiences. Stereotypical *chivalry* is a set of rigid rules for men's behavior when in the company of women, such as opening doors for them, ordering their food in a restaurant, or defending them. Some women view stereotypical chivalric behavior as offensive — they feel that it infantalizes them. Therefore, it is disrespectful to engage in these behaviors in the company of such a person. True respect is only achieved through careful attention to another person's needs and experiences. It cannot be achieved simply through the application of a rigid set of rules.

Fully Respectful Relationships

All people want respect in their relationships with others. All relationships between two people work best when the partnership has achieved high levels of mutual respect. Fully respectful relationships have the following characteristics:

- Each partner has equal influence over the activities of the partnership. Partners negotiate conflicts by asking for what they want and being willing to listen and compromise.

- Both people are equally free to speak without interruption and with the full attention of the other.

- Each person expresses positive regard for the other both in direct contact and in the company of people outside the dyad. Extremes of disrespect involve name calling, insulting, or using infantalizing terms such as referring to an adult female as a girl.

- Each person keeps private that information that he/she has agreed to keep in confidence.

- Both people can engage in constructive and respectful criticism of the other's behavior.

- Partners can disagree with each other.

- Both people can comfortably spend time away from each other and develop other kinds of relationships.

- Each partner respects the other's personal boundaries and expresses affection toward the other only with full consent.

Full consent means that there is no coercion of one partner by the other. Full consent has the following characteristics (Berkowitz 1999):

- *Both people are fully conscious.* When someone is so drunk that he or she is incapacitated, that person cannot really consent to sexual behavior.

- *Each partner is equally free to act.* A scenario in which this condition is absent: a man drives a woman to his apartment so that they can watch some videos. Afterwards, he wants to have sex but she does not. He gets angry and tells her that she can walk home, and she may either fear for her safety, or she lives too far away to walk. She might engage in sex with him because she does not like the alternatives. At the same time, she is clearly not as free to act as he is, and so there is a measure of coercion involved. We can also see a violation of this principle when one partner threatens to leave the other unless he/she has sex, or when one withdraws affection from the other based on the other's willingness to be sexual.

- *Both partners are sincere and positive in their desires.* Telling a person that you love him or her (when in fact you do not) in order to obtain permission for sex violates this principle.

- *Both partners have clearly communicated their intent.* This is difficult to achieve for some people because, although they are willing to engage in sexual behavior, they are embarrassed to talk about it. In a relationship workshop with college men, facilitators ask, "How do you know when your friend wants to kiss on a date?" Most men respond, "It's in her eyes," "she leans toward me," "it's in the air," or "I just know." Few men say, "I ask her," or "I tell her I want to kiss her and see what she says." While talking about affection and sex may feel awkward at first, it is a skill that improves with practice. To illustrate with parallels, musicians can remember how difficult it was the first time they tried to play their instruments, and athletes can remember how awkward it felt when they first tried to swing a golf club or dribble a basketball. However, these skills became second nature after a while.

Respect-disrespect is a continuum with full respect at one pole and violence, the ultimate disrespect, on the other. Somewhere on the continuum, disrespectful behaviors cross the line into illegal acts. Colleges and universities have policies regarding the disrespect of others, especially around sexual assault and sexual harassment, which also draw a line between what is allowed (but perhaps not fully respectful) and what is unacceptable. However, people should strive for fully respectful relationships, not mere compliance with law and/or campus policy. For example, it is not usually illegal or against campus policy to call other people idiots or tell them that they are ugly, but it is certainly not respectful.

Sexual Assault

Sexual assault and harassment are significant problems on college campuses and elsewhere, and perpetrators of these extreme instances of disrespect are overwhelmingly male (although most men never engage in these behaviors). The reasons for this imbalance mainly stem from men's social positions of power and the cultural masculine ethic of dominance. Sexual assault and harassment are nearly always behaviors in which a person in a powerful position exerts his/her will on a person in a less powerful position.

The stereotypical sexual-assault perpetrator is the deranged man who springs from hiding and attacks a woman somewhere outdoors. However, most sexual-assault perpetrators are men who know their victims. In most of these acquaintance rapes, perpetrator and/or victim have been drinking alcohol. However, alcohol is not the cause of the assault — there are many men who drink heavily and yet never commit a sexual assault, and people are responsible for their actions even when they are drunk.

Some perpetrators try to get their victims drunk and isolate them from others so that they can attack. Perpetrators drink to appear social, to steel themselves for the attack, to deny their responsibility for the attack ("I was drunk; it was all a misunderstanding;") and/or to blame their victims ("She was drunk, said yes when she didn't want to, and is now trying to blame me.") When an attack occurs and both victim and perpetrator are drunk at the time, people tend to blame the man less and the woman more than if both were sober.

Despite beliefs to the contrary, most sexual assaults are not the result of misunderstandings between two people; they are predatory and usually planned attacks on the part of the perpetrator. To attribute a sexual assault to miscommunication is to blame the victim and fail to hold the perpetrator fully responsible for his behavior.

Despite beliefs to the contrary, sexual assault is not the result of a failure of control over one's sexual feelings. Rather it is an act of violence. In a consensual sexual encounter, a man would stop if the couple were interrupted by others, especially the woman's parents. Therefore, men are capable of controlling their behavior even in a state of high sexual arousal. In many cases of rape, the perpetrator has to masturbate and/or force his victim into oral sex in order to get an erection. In some cases of rape, the rapist has difficulty remembering whether or not he had an orgasm (Groth 1979).

Although all men are not potential perpetrators of sexual assault, these behaviors are related to the culture of masculinity, and therefore solutions can be found in understanding and changing the negative aspects of this culture. Men have an important role to play in reducing all forms of disrespect toward women, and it is a role that goes beyond merely refraining from disrespectful behaviors. Men can encourage or discourage rape-supportive attitudes in their everyday behavior.

In order for a sexual assault to take place, at least three conditions must be present. First, there must be individual pathology on the part of the perpetrator. Research indicates that sexual-assault perpetrators tend to have the following characteristics:

- Perpetrators show more extreme acceptance of hypermasculine ideologies and higher levels of hostility toward women than nonperpetrators. This is not to say that all men who accept hypermasculine ideologies and who have high levels of hostility toward women are rapists, but all rapists seem to have these characteristics, and so these attitudes are a significant risk factor.

- Many perpetrators have feelings of having been harmed or ridiculed by women, and so their violence is connected to a motive of revenge.

- Perpetrators usually have feelings that they could not be "man enough" to suit their fathers. Again, all men who have these feelings are not perpetrators, but most perpetrators have these feelings. Men who commit sexual assault are somewhat like stereotypical schoolyard bullies. Lacking a sense of acceptance from others, they dominate others in order to feel superior. In the case of sexual-assault perpetrators, they feel unaccepted by the most important man in their lives, their fathers. Their acceptance of hypermasculine demands to never appear vulnerable prevents them from dealing with these negative feelings. As a result, they tend to convert all vulnerable emotions into anger, which is culturally acceptable for men. They then act out their emotional difficulties through violence.

- Perpetrators are more likely than nonperpetrators to subscribe to two kinds of toxic beliefs: rape myths and adversarial sexual beliefs. "Rape myths" are that "no" sometimes means "maybe" or "yes," and that women like to be forced into having sex. A rapist may confuse force with seduction and convince himself that his victim actually enjoys being overpowered. Adversarial sexual beliefs are that men and women are enemies and that a date is a kind of competition in which the man tries to get sex and the woman tries to get affection and/or get the man to spend money on her. Again, in combination with hypermasculine attitudes, the man thinks that he must go after what he wants, not take "no" for an answer, and "win" the competition.

- Perpetrators have often suffered physical, emotional, and/or sexual abuse as children, and have not dealt with this victimization in any direct way (see Lisak 1997; Lisak and Roth 1988).

- Perpetrators tend to externalize their own emotional pain and have little empathy for the pain of others.

The second condition necessary for a sexual assault is a decision on the part of the perpetrator. Regardless of individual pathology, a perpetrator makes a choice to engage in violent behavior, and he is responsible for his choice. As a parallel, a person may drive drunk because he or she has poor judgment and difficulty regulating his/her drinking, but if that person causes a car accident and hurts another human being, he/she is nevertheless accountable for the accident.

The third condition necessary for a sexual assault is cultural and social support. In some cultures, this form of violence is extremely rare or even nonexistent (Sanday 1981). In mainstream U.S. culture, sexual assault takes place in a social context in which men are encouraged to see themselves as different from and better than women. Therefore, they may feel entitled to sex and other pleasures by virtue of their status as men and view women as sexual objects whose feelings are not worthy of consideration. In male social groups, men who have impersonal sex with many different women may attain status among their friends. Men are encouraged to be ready for sex at all times and to overpower women by going after what they want and never taking "no" for an answer. Having sex with women is a way to prove that one is not gay, and so it is a way to mitigate individual and group homophobia. Men are encouraged to view sex as a set of tasks and techniques rather than a relational behavior between two people. There is also a tendency to convert all emotional experiences into anger and/or lust. Vulnerable feelings are seen as completely in control; anger and lust as being completely out of control. Sexual feelings are considered to only take place in the penis, therefore behaviors short of orgasm may be considered not good enough. Finally, masculine culture sees violence as an acceptable way to solve problems.

Despite the rape-supportive aspects of peer groups and the culture at large, most men never commit sexual assault for a variety of reasons. Most men are not violent. They respect women and do not want to hurt another human being. They want relationships with women that are based on love and affection.

How Men Can Help to Reduce Sexual Assault

Because sexual assault takes place within a culture that contains toxic characteristics within its prescriptions for masculinity, all men can help to reduce sexual assault. At the most basic level, they can do so by refusing to be perpetrators. That means that they engage in sexual behavior only with full consent and that they strive for fully respectful relationships.

Men can also use their influence on other men to decrease the likelihood of sexual assault. They can do so by modeling respect for women in their interactions with other men, by refusing to participate in cultural events that support a view of violence as masculine, such as "professional wrestling," action/adventure movies, and violent television or music. They can help to educate other men about the negative effects of such events and the ideologies that go along with them.

Men should also refuse to participate in activities that denigrate women, such as the use of pornography (especially violent pornography) and other sexual objectification, such as rating women's bodies in public, patronizing stripper bars or restaurants like "Hooters," and talking with male friends about women solely in sexual terms. They should not exhibit negative attitudes toward women in sexist humor or by using terms that animalize ("bitch," "fox"), dehumanize ("whore," "slut") or infantalize ("girl," "baby") women. They should never laugh or otherwise give their approval when men behave in sexist ways. Doing so requires a consciousness that this kind of negative talk can hurt other people even if they do not hear it. Many people have attained this consciousness with regard to racist humor and put-downs (although clearly, many have not), and we must apply the same mentality to sexism, homophobia, and other forms of inequality. Men should refuse to participate when men challenge other men's masculinity by using antifemininity ("Take off your skirt and play like a man."), homophobia ("Only a fag wouldn't have another shot of liquor."), or masculine shame ("What are you, a wus?"). They should never brag about sexual conquest or approve of other men who brag.

Men can be especially helpful by refusing to condone dangerous attitudes by being a passive bystander when male friends behave in sexist ways, even when no women are present. Challenging male friends who behave in such ways involves several steps (Berkowitz 1999):

He must notice the sexist behavior. Negative attitudes toward women can be very obvious, such as name-calling or other hateful speech, or it can be more subtle, such as referring to adult females as "girls" or frequently interrupting them.

He must see the behavior as a problem that affects him personally. If a man realizes the full impact of hypermasculinity on his own life, he cannot disconnect the attitudes of his friends from his own desires and needs.

He must take responsibility for doing something about the problem. If he views the bystander role as a neutral one, then he may feel comfortable with remaining silent. However, if he understands that the bystander role condones and even encourages the disrespect of women, he may feel more compelled to speak up.

He must have the skills to intervene. Men who are committed to this course of action must develop influential ways of talking to other men that fit their style and their relationships with these men.

Doing this work requires courage, leadership, independence, orientation toward action, and risk-taking, all of which are positive traditionally masculine attributes. It takes a good deal of effort to learn about gender and masculinity, to embrace gender-based violence as a "men's issue," and to make conscious choices about one's behaviors rather than blindly conforming to gender stereotypes. College men who want to involve themselves in this work in formal ways should consider joining or founding a peer-education program and/or participating in consciousness raising and social change efforts to decrease men's gender-based violence. These efforts include the White Ribbon Campaign and the Men's Rape Prevention Project, in which men educate others about the problem of men's violence against women. (Resources for learning about these efforts are in Appendix A.)

Breaking the Pressure to Blindly Conform to Gender Stereotypes

Men receive a great deal of social pressure to behave in hypermasculine ways, yet most men are kind and sensitive people who do not fit the cultural stereotype. At the same time, most men overestimate the degree to which other men are comfortable with sexism and other hypermasculine behavior. This distorted judgment of other men occurs because men compare their inner *reactions* to other men's *appearances*. In a typical scenario, a group of men are conversing, and one of them makes a disrespectful, perhaps even violent comment about a woman. All the men in the room laugh, which indicates approval for the comment. It is easy to assume that these men's public approval also indicates private approval. However, most of these men are going along with the joke because they want to be part of the group, not because they like what the disrespectful man is saying. An individual man in the group feels uncomfortable, but when he looks around the room, all of the other men appear to be quite comfortable. It is likely that many of them are not, but he would never know that unless they told him so. When he compares his inner feeling of discomfort with their outward appearance of comfort, he feels like a misfit. Therefore, he is unlikely to challenge the negative attitude being displayed because he fears that doing so will break the "masculine code" and result in his being ostracized from the rest of the group.

Understanding these gender forces frees men to discover who they truly are and to make affirmative choices about their behaviors and attitudes rather than conforming to culturally based gender stereotypes. In the process, they may inspire and help other men to do the same. It isn't necessary to give an elaborate speech in order to display disapproval for another man's sexism. Sometimes, simply saying, "Hey — have some respect for the woman." can make a powerful statement. When offered pornography, a man can say, "I don't want that to be a part of my life."

A number of situational factors can empower men to break the sexist conformity of stereotypical men's social groups. An especially powerful one is the perception that one has at least one ally in the group. Classic studies on conformity indicate that group members are much more willing to speak up against the majority opinion when it is not unanimous (Asch 1965). Knowing that he has a tendency to overestimate the level of others' approval of sexism, a man is more likely to perceive an ally and therefore to break conformity. If he takes this leadership role (a masculine attribute) by disagreeing, he frees other men to express a dissenting opinion as well. Preliminary research indicates that simply knowing that one has a tendency to overestimate other men's comfort is effective in reducing that overestimation (Kilmartin, Conway, Friedberg, McQuoid, and Tschan 1999).

When men understand that the bystander role is not neutral, that hypermasculinity and sexism are toxic, and that they have an important influence on their peers, they can begin to accept responsibility for their behavior within the social group. Because negative attitudes toward women are damaging to the person who holds and expresses these attitudes, challenging him is a way of caring for a friend. The easiest part of being a friend is going along with the other person when he does something you like or agree with. It is more difficult to challenge him when he is being self-destructive and disrespectful. Many men think that remaining silent in these situations means being loyal to a friend, when in reality it is extremely disloyal.

It is crucial to establish a presence of appropriate models of healthy masculine behaviors. Unless men know that there are alternatives to blind conformity to hypermasculinity, they will not be able to understand that other choices are available. Despite the fact that independence is a masculine attribute, independence to gender pressure is still a rare commodity.

Most people realize that we look to our attitudes to shape our behaviors, but it is also true that we look to our behaviors to shape our attitudes. Taking a behavioral course of action strengthens the attitude. Therefore, providing ways in which men can publicly display respectful attitudes toward women will reinforce their private acceptance of the attitude. Challenging a hypermasculine behavior makes it more likely that one will think it important to do so, and it will also help men to further develop the skills to intervene again.

The Value of Gender Awareness

In summary, there are a number of important rewards for becoming gender aware. Men who do so attain more freedom of choice about their goals, behaviors, and attitudes. They take fewer risks with their physical and mental well-being, and so they are likely to live longer and healthier lives. They can achieve more rewarding relationships of all kinds by taking on the culturally defined feminine attributes of empathy and connectedness. They will experience a fuller emotional life and increased opportunities for success in all areas of their lives.

3
Strategies for Delivery

There are many different ways to deliver the content of gender-aware programs described in Chapter 2. How you do so on your campus will depend on a number of considerations. In beginning to implement a program for men or in re-evaluating an existing program, you might ask yourself the following questions:

- (?) What resources (e.g., time, money, expertise, personnel, space) are available for this effort? What additional resources might we pursue, and how would we do so?

- (?) To what extent are influential people on campus (e.g., president, deans, athletic director, coaches, Greek affairs personnel) sympathetic to the problem? What might we do to increase their commitment to addressing gender issues for men, especially sexual assault?

- (?) Are there interested faculty or staff with backgrounds in men's issues and the willingness to help? If so, what are the possibilities for utilizing their time and for compensating them?

- (?) Are campus visitors (e.g., consultants, guest speakers) a possibility? If so, which ones might be most suited to our campus atmosphere, and how can we maximize their effectiveness?

(?) How can we compel men to participate in gender-aware education? What existing groups of men (e.g., fraternities, athletic teams, interest groups) constitute ready-made audiences for gender-aware education? How can we gain entry into these groups?

(?) What colleagues on other campuses have these kinds of programs? How might they be able to inform our programs?

(?) If we get students involved in doing the education (which is highly recommended), how can we motivate them to participate? Are there enough students who will volunteer and follow through? Can we pay them? Can we arrange academic credit?

(?) How will we deal with resistance from men who feel threatened by this approach? How can we build the credibility of our offices/programs?

(?) How can we communicate concern for men and hold them responsible for their behavior at the same time?

(?) What long-range goals and plans do we have in mind?

The answers to these questions will shape the approach of the individual campus to providing services for men. At the beginning stages, groups of professionals and students should meet to discuss these questions and others that seem relevant. Following are some guidelines for designing your programs.

Basic Advice

Think Developmentally and Develop Long-Range Plans

Campus programming does not simply appear on the scene. It changes and (hopefully) grows as we develop resources and allies, learn from experience, discover new methods, and respond to the changing needs and character of our campus cultures. Therefore, it is crucial to develop a vision of how programs will develop over the years and to re-evaluate one's goals on a yearly basis. At a minimum, such long-range plans should identify:

- goals and objectives,
- targeted service delivery (e.g., number of programs delivered, attendance, groups addressed),
- personnel responsible for programming,
- staff development (workshops, conferences, meetings),
- material resources needed,
- methods for program evaluation, and
- program growth year to year.

Evaluate Current Programs and Campus Atmosphere

A starting point for long-range planning is an evaluation of the state-of-current-service delivery. The stage model of program development in Chapter 1 may be helpful in assessing the state of current programming and setting realistic short- and long-term goals. Unless the campus is willing to commit considerable resources to the effort, it is probably not realistic to move from ground zero to fully integrated programming within a year or two. However, one might discover possibilities for moving from Stage 1 to Stage 2 or 3 within a relatively brief time period.

An evaluation of campus atmosphere is critical to program design. It may be a major victory to bring in a one-shot program to a military school that is only recently gender-integrated, or to do a single program with fraternities or athletic teams whose leaders are unsympathetic to the importance of doing gender education with males. It usually will be slower to develop elaborate programming on campuses that have never done anything to address the gendered context of male sexual assault or those in which there are few allies in powerful positions. This is not to say that plans should not be ambitious, but that they need to take into account the history and culture of the campus.

Use Multiple Groups to Evaluate and Plan Programs

Students, faculty, administrators, and staff often have different perspectives on what exists and what is needed. Therefore, it is important to understand these multiple perspectives in designing your approach. One strategy is to construct a task force that includes participation from multiple constituencies. Another is to arrange activities such as focus groups or evaluation sessions with students, especially male students. These activities might take place in the original planning stages, and/or they might be used to view and respond to existing programs or proposals. If students do not bring a high level of investment to the causes of the programming group (i.e., they are merely given course credit for participating in the focus group), highly structured activities are usually more useful than open-ended discussions. For example, you might assemble a group of male students to view a videotape of the approach you are considering and have them complete questionnaires detailing their reactions. Then, you can introduce structured questions in a focus group to stimulate discussion of the approach.

Enter Existing Groups of Men and Captive Audiences

Especially at the early stages of program development, it is not likely that offering a program with solely voluntary attendance will be highly successful at reaching a large male audience. However, it might be useful in identifying men who are highly committed to gender education and enlisting them as allies, an important goal for program development.

It is easier to gain entry into groups and settings that already exist on the campus. At most colleges and universities, these include: fraternities, athletic teams, the classroom, first-year student orientation, speaker series' with mandatory attendance or a menu of attendance options, residence-hall programs, clubs, or course credit given by instructors for student attendance. Using these avenues of access has at least three advantages. First, it obviously provides a measure of incentive for attending the program. Second, it allows men who are interested in gender to come to the program without having themselves or others worry about their masculinity, as gendered thinking is culturally defined as unmasculine. Third, it gives men who regularly interact with one another a shared experience that may open the door for positive peer influence, especially if follow-up activities encourage those kinds of interactions.

You might worry that men will attend in order to meet some requirement, but then refuse to pay attention to the material being delivered. My experience in over 15 years of programming with men is that they tend to be vitally interested in learning about masculinity, as it is central to their feelings about themselves. Talented presenters will have little difficulty in engaging their attention. It may be one of the very few times that anyone talks to them about masculinity, a cultural force that has a great deal of influence on them. The most difficult part of men's programming is getting the men into the room where the program is to take place, thus the captive audience affords a unique opportunity of access. The gender-aware approach has a much greater potential to engage men than a narrower sexual-assault program, as it addresses such an important part of their experience.

Enter the Power Structure at the Highest Level Possible

In seeking resources, try to find the most powerful person who is sympathetic (or at least open) to providing gender education for men. Ideally, this would be the president of the college. Alternately (or additionally), the dean of students, athletic director, coaches, residence-life director, or Greek affairs personnel can be instrumental both in dedicating time, personnel, and funds, and in facilitating entry into male audiences.

In the initial stages of "selling" this approach to less-than-sympathetic administrators, you should avoid using moral arguments. Although sexual assault is obviously a moral issue, subtly or overtly telling an administrator that failing to implement these programs would mean that he or she is a bad person will usually result in more opposition. Talk their language: recruitment, retention, reputation, and liability. Emphasize both the positive aspects of implementing and improving programs and the negative aspects of not doing so. Talk about how this kind of programming fits within the central missions of the college.

Aim Toward Maximum Use of Male Peers

In the beginning stages of implementation, it may be very difficult to find the necessary resources to launch a peer-education program. However, such a program should be in your long-range plan. Research indicates that well-trained peer educators are more successful at persuasion than faculty, staff, or guests. They have a credibility that even the most talented older presenter does not — audience members can see age peers as similar to themselves. In addition, peer educators can be positive role models in their everyday interactions with other men.

Avoid "Real-Man" Approaches

It is tempting to use traditional masculinity to gain men's attention and to motivate them to comply. For instance, a presenter might use a sports metaphor to talk about dating, such as, "Don't get into the game if you're not in shape." Some campuses have asked prominent males on campus to sign a pledge that they will not assault a woman. Then they publish their names in the school newspaper with the heading, "These are the "Real Men" of Central University." (Note that all men were not asked to sign, that no proactive behavior on the part of these men is necessary for their inclusion, and that merely signing a piece of paper elevates them to the status of "Real Men.")

These kinds of approaches have a number of disadvantages. First, they reinforce a hypermasculine ideology, which is a risk factor for sexual assault. Second, they do not really facilitate men's appreciation of alternate models of masculinity. Most importantly, they shame and undignify men who do not participate by suggesting that they are not worthwhile. Shame is an emotion that underlies disrespectful behavior. All men are "real" and deserve their dignity.

Use Interactive and Structured Approaches

Research indicates that the most successful programs are interactive in nature. Lectures may be useful, but they should be accompanied by discussions of the material. For most men, thinking of themselves as gendered beings is a very new experience. They tend to be overwhelmed with this new and important information, and it is difficult for them to articulate a response in an open-ended, unstructured discussion. Therefore, questions used in discussions should provide a structure that allows them to focus on a particular aspect of the presentation. Writing exercises and structured questionnaires may also be useful in helping them to find a starting point for processing the information.

Begin in Single-Sex Groups

At the beginning stages, raising consciousness is best undertaken in homogenous groups. It is uncomfortable and intimidating for men to begin learning about gender when women are present. Women tend to have a good deal more experience in this area (as gender is highlighted in their everyday lives) and thus they are more likely to have articulate responses to the material. Men will be less likely to speak freely for fear of offending women and may also perform in order to attract women. Intergender dialogue can proceed in later programming.

You may encounter significant resistance in trying to separate the sexes for this kind of programming. Others may worry that men are being "singled out" and regarded as perpetrators. Try to "sell" this approach with the argument that, in the case of sexual-assault programming, men and women have somewhat different educational needs, and that research indicates that single-sex programs are preferable, especially when introducing the material (Earle 1992). Mixed-sex programs are clearly better than no program at all — you may have to begin with them if the resistance to single-sex programs is too great. You may also be able to do both mixed-sex and single-sex programs.

Use Multiple Modes of Education

A variety of approaches to delivery of educational material facilitates participants' information processing. At a minimum, men should have the opportunity to do so both publicly, as in a discussion, and privately, as in a writing exercise. Multiple modes of presentation and response reduce boredom and allow participants the opportunity to fit the material into their distinctive learning styles. Some possibilities are: discussions, questionnaires, films, theatrical presentations, writing exercises, role playing, and values clarification exercises. Interactive drama may be especially useful in facilitating information processing by participants (Heppner Humphrey, Hillenbrand-Gunn, and DeBord 1995).

Responding to Frequently Asked Questions

Well-trained presenters have a solid background in the issues surrounding their subject matter, and they have articulate statements ready to respond to questions from their audiences. They should undergo extensive training that includes reading (Appendix A contains some suggestions for reading material) and practice at presenting. In the early stages, they should be supervised by more experienced presenters. Following are some sample responses to questions that male college students frequently ask during gender-aware, sexual-assault presentations. I present general questions on gender first and specific ones on sexual assault later.

Aren't men and women different because of biology? Biology undoubtedly plays a role in behavior, but it does so by setting thresholds for behaviors that are then restrained or encouraged by social forces. For example, the brain is structured to acquire language, but which language a child acquires is obviously a product of the language that he or she is exposed to at an early age. In most cases, research indicates that there are small or insignificant differences in the behaviors of men and women. Even in cases where there are differences, these are small, average differences and not large differences that apply to every male or every female (with the exception of the reproductive behaviors: impregnation, gestation, lactation, and menstruation). Everywhere we see sex differences, there are wide variations *within* the group of men and *within* the group of women. For example, men as a group are more violent than women as a group, but some women are violent and most men are not violent. Moreover, women are known to display *aggression* just as frequently as men, but they are more likely than men to display it verbally. Cross-cultural research demonstrates the powerful effect of culture on social ideologies, including those that surround gender, and the behaviors that affect these ideologies. Biology is important, but human beings are, more than any other animals, creatures of our experience.

Isn't this all oversensitive, politically correct (p.c.), feminist garbage? Oversensitivity as a problem pales in comparison to undersensitivity. If it is a matter of taking a little extra time to consider another person's feelings before acting as opposed to losing a little of one's spontaneity, it would seem to be preferable to err on the side of oversensitivity. P.C. is a pejorative term invented to make sensitive people feel badly about their sensitivity. If you can substitute the term "respectful" for P.C. in the sentence, then the term is misplaced. We also see socially conservative people vilifying and devaluing others' identities. The term "feminist" is a good case in point. The term merely means a person who believes that women should have equal political, social, and economic opportunities to men (and there is a great deal of diversity of opinions among feminists). But for many people, the term has come to be understood as an ideology held by women who hate men and want to overpower them. While gender awareness and sexual-assault prevention are feminist in nature, they fit the former, not the latter definition.

Wouldn't everything just be simpler if we went back to a time when men and women had well-defined roles? Perhaps it would, but for whom, and at what price? The bottom line of gender relations is that, regardless of how much we might like to return to the idyllic world of the 1950s (which were not as great for most people as the romanticized recollections of that period), the needs of our societies will not support rigid gender arrangements. Therefore, clinging to the old ways will come at increasing costs in the modern world, just as it will for those who refuse to learn how to use a computer or wear seat belts. The use of a person's status as male or female to narrowly define their possibilities in life is an enormous waste of individual potential. Change is usually accompanied by discomfort. The unease we may feel with changing gender is more the result of "growing pains" than an indication that something is fundamentally wrong.

I really want to be closer to my father. How do I do it? (First, a presenter should praise the courage of a man who asks such a question. Many men want to be closer to their fathers, but rarely do they talk about it, as hyperindependence is a defining feature of masculinity. A presenter should make note that the questioner's concern is a common one, thus giving other audience members permission to voice the same concern. One possible way of responding):

Of course, I don't know your father, so it is difficult for me to say with any certainty what will work with him. But I can give you some general advice. People become closer when they disclose experiences to one another, especially when these experiences involve the inner life of vulnerable or tender emotions. So your tasks are to do so yourself and to get your dad to do so. Story telling is one activity in which many men have experience and skills. In order to become closer to one another, we have to tell our stories in a different way. When you tell your stories to your father, try to think about your emotional responses to the events you are describing and include them in your story. Use words that describe how you felt, e.g., sad, happy, worried, afraid, sentimental, in addition to those that describe what took place and what you thought.

You might be able to get your father to tell his stories by finding some time alone with him, perhaps in the course of doing some activity like taking a walk or fishing together, and by being curious about some aspect of his life. For example, you might ask, "What was it like to be in the Army?" or "Tell me about how you met Mom." When he tells the story, you can be curious about his emotional responses to the events he is describing, thus encouraging him to elaborate upon his inner life. If you are successful, you will get to know each other better and hopefully become closer in the process. You can use the same kinds of strategies to get closer to your male friends.

If men have so much power, why don't I feel powerful? For a couple of reasons: first, power is not distributed to all men in equal shares. Men who are not wealthy, attractive, athletic, or in the ethnic majority are not usually as powerful as men who have these attributes. Because they tend to have less money and formal power than older men, younger men tend to have less overall power. Second, masculinity is culturally defined as a deficit situation. It is impossible to be "number one" all of the time, yet masculinity demands it of us and highlights what we do not have rather than what we do have. (This is why a critical understanding of the cultural pressures of masculinity will free us to make wiser choices about our lives and enrich our understanding of and comfort with ourselves.) Third, and most importantly, privilege is usually invisible to the person who holds it unless you call his or her attention to it. Few of us wake up on a cold winter morning and think about the fact that our houses are heated and others' houses are not. In the gender realm, few men think about the facts that most people will take us seriously, that we are unlikely to be followed or harassed in public, that the vast majority of the people in power are the same gender as we are, that our experience is seen as the standard, not the exception, and that other people are likely to attribute our successes and failures to our efforts, rather than to the fact that we are male.

Are you saying that men should be like women? No. I am saying that men need to take a critical look at the cultural expectations that masculinity provides and make informed choices about their behavior rather than merely "going along with the program." It is difficult to resist the program when you don't understand it, and therefore it is critically important that men learn about gender if we are to reach our full potentials. We need to consider possibilities in ourselves that may step outside of traditional masculinity, to expand our options beyond the narrow ones defined by outdated modes of gender.

Is it fair for a man to be accused of rape just because he has had a misunderstanding with a woman? You are responsible for obtaining consent from somebody before engaging in any sexual behaviors with him or her. If a man has assaulted a woman without being aware that he has, he is still responsible for his actions. To illustrate a parallel situation: if I were to leave my golf clubs on my front porch and someone were to take them, it would be theft regardless of whether the thief defined it as such.

We should be careful not to assume that most rapes are the result of mere miscommunication. They are not. Most rapes are the result of predatory behavior on the part of the perpetrator, who plans to isolate the victim, sometimes incapacitate him or her with alcohol or other drugs, and then attack. And while such a person might consider himself charming or seductive, he is still offensive, assaultive, and illegal.

As long as I don't rape somebody, what does this have to do with me? We like to believe that rape is a behavior that is the product of an individual's sick mind. It is, but it is also a behavior that is encouraged or discouraged by others (recall that rape is very rare or even nonexistent in some cultures). Therefore, men have a responsibility to the society to not support the negative attitudes toward women that underlie rape and to challenge those attitudes when they run across them.

An example of another hate crime will serve to illustrate. There is a long history of African Americans being murdered by whites simply because they are of a different color. The vast majority of whites would never consider doing so, but when they behave in racist ways, they encourage people at the extreme to engage in racist violence. The murderer hates people of color, and this attitude has been supported by other racist people who have never committed an overt act of violence. If the attitude did not exist, the crime would not have been committed. It is the same with sexual assault and the hatred of women, and men have an especially important role to play because they have influence with other men.

Men can also be victims of rape, and they are also frequently "secondary victims," meaning that they have been harmed by an assault on a friend, lover, or family member. For example, a girlfriend might be mistrustful, sexually inhibited, angry with men in general, or otherwise emotionally vulnerable because she has been assaulted, and this is sure to affect relationships. And, of course, it is very painful to witness the suffering of someone you love.

Aren't women the powerful ones, because they can falsely accuse us of rape? You might ask yourself, "Have *I* ever falsely accused someone of wrongdoing because I felt hurt or I was angry with him or her?" "If so, how far did I follow through with the accusation?" "If I followed through, did the truth come out in the end?" People do not tend to make rape accusations lightly. It takes a great deal of time, effort, and emotional upheaval to follow an accusation through the legal process or even a campus policy hearing. While false accusations are not unheard of, they are a very small minority. Very few people are so vindictive or driven by dominance that they would go to this extreme. False accusations are much more the stuff of soap operas and movies than real life occurrences.

Does alcohol cause sexual assault? In a large proportion of sexual assaults on college campuses, perpetrator and/or victim had used alcohol, often to excess, prior to the assault. Alcohol helps the perpetrator to subdue his victim and may also be used by the perpetrator to summon his nerve to commit the crime. Obviously, alcohol also undermines one's judgment, making it more likely that a perpetrator will commit the crime and more likely that a victim will place herself in a risky situation. However, to say that alcohol *causes* sexual assault would be entirely wrong. Many men have drunk to excess and never committed a sexual assault. To say that a person was assaulted because he or she got drunk is to blame the victim. A natural consequence of drinking too much is a hangover, not becoming a victim of a crime.

Talking about sex before having it is really uncomfortable. How can you expect us to do that? Clear sexual communication involves a set of skills, and skills improve with practice. If you are a musician or an athlete, you may remember the first time, e.g., you tried to dribble a basketball with your left hand or play a scale on the piano. It felt very awkward, but if you stuck with it, you got better at it — so much so that it became second nature. If we waited to feel completely comfortable before doing, there would be few difficult things ever accomplished. The key is not to wait until you feel comfortable; it is to act despite feeling uncomfortable because the outcome is important to you. Comfort will come with familiarity and practice. You practiced your sport or music because it was important to you. Respectful relationships are very important to nearly everybody. Contrary to popular belief, they are not just a matter of meeting the right person — you have to work at them.

What about women who tease men by getting them aroused sexually and then refusing to go all the way? Men are entitled to feelings about such women and should deal with these feelings in whatever responsible way is helpful to them. However, women (and men, for that matter) always have the right to refuse to engage in sexual behavior and to withdraw their consent at any time. If a person withdraws consent and the other person continues without that consent, it is sexual assault.

One prevalent myth is that men cannot stop themselves once they become highly aroused. But men can do so. Imagine this scenario: you are a heterosexual man at your girlfriend's house ready to have (consensual) sex with her on the living room sofa. At the moment just before intercourse is to take place, her parents return home unexpectedly. Most men would have no problem bringing their behavior under control.

These answers are only provided as general assistance at thinking about issues connected to the subject matter. They are not formulaic responses that presenters should memorize and repeat word for word. And they only touch on many deeper and more complicated issues. Therefore, you might think of these responses to frequently asked questions as ways of stimulating further discussion, not as ending the discussion at hand. Presenters would do well to engage in such discussions among themselves in order to find their own voices and further their thinking about the issues.

Three Great Ideas for Involving Men in Anti-Violence Work

In addition to specific educational programs, it is possible to raise male consciousness about gender issues with environmental interventions aimed at changing the campus social atmosphere. Following are descriptions of three such programs that have met with a degree of success at colleges and universities.

The Social-Norms Approach

The social-norms approach is a strategy for reducing men's sexism toward women. Male sexism is a risk factor for sexual assault, and so reducing it serves the goal of prevention as well as the positive goal of improving respectful relationships between the sexes. Despite the traditional ideology of men as independent, there is a great deal of conformity in men's peer groups. When men make sexist comments or jokes, other men are pressured to laugh along with the group, or at least to remain silent. These behaviors condone or encourage the attitude that is on display. Men who challenge other men's sexism risk being ostracized from the social group.

Some research evidence suggests that most college men are uncomfortable when other men make comments that endorse coercive sexuality, refer to women by animal names or the names of women's genitals, publicly rate women's bodies, or make wolf whistles and catcalls as women pass by in public space (Berkowitz 1994; Kilmartin, Conway, Friedberg, McQuoid, and Tschan 1999). Yet they tend to underestimate other men's discomfort because they compare their private experience with other men's overt behavior. When they do so, they perceive themselves as being more sensitive than their friends. Therefore, they tend to remain silent because they fear that they will be ostracized from the social group if they challenge these behaviors. However, classic social psychological research indicates that the perception of even a single ally is an important factor in breaking group conformity (Asch 1965). Thus, changes in perception can empower men to challenge the sexist behavior of their peers.

Because a distortion of the estimated attitude of the group maintains the negative behavior, a correction of that distortion is thought to be a critical step in changing the behavior. The social-norms approach entails the use of public information campaigns to change the perception of the norm. This approach has been successful with the problem of college binge drinking. College students overestimate how much other students drink and try to conform to the perceived norm. When researchers conduct surveys of student drinking and publicize the results in credible fashion, student binge drinking decreases (Haines 1997).

Applying this approach to men's sexism, the first step is to conduct a survey of men's comfort/discomfort with other men's sexism. Obtain access to a sample of men on campus (for instance, through the psychology department's research participant pool) and have them fill out a survey that presents a variety of scenarios in which men are behaving in sexist ways in all-male peer groups. For each scenario, ask them to rate their level of comfort/discomfort. Most research like this employs a seven-point scale, with a rating of "one" as "extremely comfortable" and a rating of "seven" as "extremely uncomfortable." Then, ask them to rate a male friend and/or "the average male student on this campus" across the same scenarios. Taken together, the self-ratings are a measure of the average male student's comfort/discomfort if the sample is representative of the population. These ratings should be significantly higher, i.e., indicate greater discomfort, than the estimation of other men's comfort/discomfort.

The next step is to publicize the results. You can do so using fliers, posters, campus radio or television messages, school newspaper advertisements, e-mail, websites, tee shirts, key chains, pens, bookmarks, or other communications available on your campus. Take care to develop credible and memorable messages to publicize. Student focus groups can be helpful in designing these messages, which should be simple and straightforward. For instance, a poster might say, "Seventy-five percent of all male students at Central University are uncomfortable when men make derogatory comments about women. Speak up and challenge this kind of talk when you hear it."

Social norms experts Alan Berkowitz, Michael Haines, Koreen Johannessen, and Jeff Linkenbach provide the following suggestions for undertaking a media campaign (*Health Education Section Newsletter,* American College Health Association, Fall 1998).

- Do your homework. You will need to do some research to determine your own campus norms, where your students receive their information, and what images they identify with.

- All messages should be positive (promote achievable behaviors), inclusive (include all elements of target population), and empowering (affirm and encourage rather than scare and blame).

- Tell the truth and provide the sources for the statistics you use.

- Use normative behavior (that which more than 50 percent do). Focus on normalizing protective behaviors, not denormalizing negative behaviors.

- Use one main message. Tie supporting messages to your main message.

- Feedback from students is critical. Use student focus groups to determine which messages are most memorable, and most favorably received.

- Make the ads visually appealing. Photographs of students tend to work well. Match the photo to the message.

- Use multiple forms of media.

- Realize that every campus is different, and each will require a slightly (or radically) different approach. Messages and media that work well on a commuter campus with high newspaper readership may differ from those that work on a residential campus with a popular campus radio station.

- Don't expect immediate results. Believability and recognition comes with time.

The next step is to undertake research to evaluate the effectiveness of the media campaign. This step involves administering the original survey to the same or a new group of male students. A successful campaign should result in a decrease in the gap between self-ratings and estimations of other men's comfort/discomfort.

The social-norms approach is not the be-all and end-all of sexual-assault prevention, but it can be a valuable addition to other efforts. Men's beliefs that they are not alone in their sensitivity do not necessarily lead to changes in their behavior, but they are a key ingredient. Men also need to learn that the passive-bystander role is not neutral, to take responsibility for undertaking a course of action, and to gain the ability to intervene effectively. The social-norms approach can build the necessary perception, and other education can address the cognitive understanding and skill acquisition that comprise the other essential components of the formula. Because most men behave in sexist ways in order to gain the approval of other men, the withdrawal of that approval can go a long way in the efforts to change toxic beliefs and behaviors.

The White Ribbon Campaign

In December 1991, Canadian men of conscience launched the White Ribbon Campaign in response to the 1990 "Montreal Massacre," when a male engineering student murdered 14 women at the *L'ecole Polytechnique* in Montreal before committing suicide. These killings were clearly gender-related — the murderer blamed women for his lack of academic success and narrowed career opportunities. In his words, "Feminists ruined my life."

The campaign was an effort to get men to show their support for ending men's violence against women. Activists distributed white ribbons at schools, churches, shops, and places of employment. As the campaign became highly visible, men's violence against women became a subject for publicity, discussion, and debate. During recent White Ribbon weeks, an estimated one in nine Canadian men were wearing the ribbons, including the Prime Minister and other prominent national figures. The larger goal, to develop a nationwide men's antiviolence network, is well underway (Sluser and Kaufman 1992). The White Ribbon Campaign is the first large-scale initiative ever developed by men to speak out on a subject usually considered to be a "women's issue."

An important aspect of the campaign is the raising of money for rape-crisis centers, domestic-violence shelters, and batterer-treatment programs. As the campaign became highly visible, men's violence against women became a subject for publicity, discussion, and debate. Many men across Canada were talking seriously about the problem for the first time.

I brought the White Ribbon Campaign to my campus in 1994, and it has since spread to many colleges and universities in the United States. The campaign has four broad goals:

- to raise awareness of the social problem of men's violence against women,
- to encourage men to accept responsibility for contributing to a decrease in this violence,
- to stimulate men to discuss the issue with other men, and
- to raise money for organizations that deal directly with the consequences of men's violence against women.

The White Ribbon Campaign is an inexpensive undertaking that requires little more than a time commitment from men on campus who are interested in doing this important work in the service of social change. Following are some suggestions for launching this effort:

- Choose a week in mid-semester when course schedules and campus events allow the campaign to get the attention of the campus community (The Canadian effort is on the anniversary of the Montreal Massacre, which is the first week of December — a difficult time for most campuses because of exam schedules and the end of the semester).

- Obtain a "starter kit" and other materials from the Canadian White Ribbon office (see Appendix A).

- You can obtain rolls of white ribbon and safety pins very inexpensively. Prior to the campaign, volunteers can cut and assemble the ribbons. Note that the ribbon is simply folded over to form an upside-down "V," not looped as AIDS ribbons are. Distribute the ribbons to men on your campus. You should target high-profile men such as (if they are male) the college president, deans, athletic director, coaches, faculty members, student leaders, etc., and convince them to wear ribbons during the week. Ideally, ribbon distribution is interpersonal — men approach other men whom they know and ask them to wear the ribbon as their personal pledge never to commit, condone, or remain silent about men's violence against women. Alternately (or in addition), you can make ribbons and information available in public areas of the campus and/or send them through campus mail to male faculty, staff, and students.

- Have men sign pledge cards and/or a large white ribbon displayed in a central campus location as a public statement of support for men ending men's violence against women.

- Try to gain publicity for the problem through local and/or campus radio stations, television, newspapers, and electronic and other media.

- Post facts about men's violence against women on e-mail and in places around the campus (We post one new fact about the problem on each day of the week.) Be sure to use the active voice — say, "Every year in the United States, 1,500 men murder their female partners or ex-partners" rather than "Every year in the United States, 1,500 women are murdered by their partners or ex-partners." The emphasis is on the perpetrators' behavior.

- Plan several educational programs for the week. If you have some funding, you can bring in a national or regional expert as a guest speaker. Faculty members may have some expertise in the issue and might be willing to give a public talk and/or dedicate a class to the topic and open the class to the public. Volunteers can read poetry or essays on the topic in a public area and/or hold a vigil. One year, we put 1,500 white ribbons around a central area of campus as a graphic reminder of the problem of men's murders of their partners. Do anything that will raise awareness about the problem.

- Include in your educational programs information about the continuum of disrespect toward women and give men information about how they can help, e.g., by challenging other men who behave in sexist ways and learning more about masculinity and violence. It is also helpful for people to know that the culture of violence is supported when, e.g., people pay money to see action-adventure movies, buy products from commercial sponsors of "professional wrestling" (which is neither professional nor wrestling) and other violent television, or express the ideology that violence is an effective way to solve problems.

- Raise some money for local organizations that deal directly with men's violence against women. You can do so in a number of ways: finding some entertainers to do a benefit performance, raffling off donated items, soliciting donations, holding a bake sale, etc.

- Try to grow the campaign into a men's organization that will continue the work on an ongoing basis.

Our research indicated that students' awareness of the problem of men's violence against women and their attitude toward the problem both improved as a direct result of the White Ribbon Campaign (Kilmartin, Chirico, and Leemann 1997). This effort is significant in that it is a grass-roots movement by men in the direction of dealing with a central men's social issue. It provides a stimulus for men to begin to understand the impact of gender socialization and sexist culture on their lives.

It is obvious that people look to their attitudes to shape their behavior, but it is not so obvious that people also look to their behavior in shaping their attitudes. Social psychological research has demonstrated the "Principle of Commitment" — that publicly committing to a course of behavior increases one's private acceptance of the attitudes that support that behavior (Mayer, Duval, and Duval 1980). Men who participate in the White Ribbon Campaign may well increase their sensitivity to the problem of men's violence against women.

The Fraternity Violence Education Project

Dr. Deborah Mahlstedt of West Chester University (PA) has developed an innovative program for involving fraternity men in working against sexism and gender-based violence (See Appendix A for Dr. Mahlstedt's contact information). The approach is one of changing the organization with an influential minority of members. A small group of fraternity men participate in a full year training program on gender-based violence in exchange for academic credit and leadership skills training. Then they act as peer educators in their fraternities as well as in the Greek system in general to:

- carry prevention messages,
- serve as positive role models,
- be resources for ongoing dialogue, and
- influence other men in a positive way when potentially dangerous situations arise.

In the fall semester, these men take a seminar on violence against women for academic credit. They learn extensively about the problem, reflect on their own behavior, and learn how to facilitate group discussions. Together with one other seminar participant, they co-lead workshops and discussions in their own fraternities during the spring. The content of the program is described extensively in Dr. Mahlstedt's publication, which is cited in Appendix A. It is very much an approach consistent with this book — discussions of power and gender as the contexts of the problem of sexual assault. These discussions emphasize:

- the continuum of violence against women,
- its effect on all men and women, not just perpetrators and victims/survivors,
- a social change approach to eliminating it, and
- an emphasis on men taking responsibility for doing so.

Men are motivated to take part in the program for at least four reasons:

- compensation (course credit),
- leadership development,
- personal experience (they may know perpetrators and/or survivors, and/or be perpetrators or survivors themselves), and
- campus-wide visibility for themselves and their fraternities.

Men who participate in this training learn and teach both from personal and intellectual viewpoints. Like the White Ribbon Campaign, participants tend to become more committed to social change both by learning about the extent and implications of the problem, and by observing and processing the changes in their own behavior. The Fraternity Violence Education Project is an excellent example of several effective characteristics of men's programs: peer education, going through existing (and high-risk) campus organizations, and providing a gendered context to the problem of violence against women.

Conclusion

Effective gender-aware, sexual-assault programming is delivered to men in a way that both affects their attitudes toward women and helps them to learn about themselves. It develops over time and is energized by new resources, re-evaluation of existing programs, commitment, and creativity. Alan Berkowitz, an independent consultant to campuses on sexual assault, suggests that the most effective programs have the following characteristics:

- comprehensiveness — good programs involve all campus constituencies and addresses bystander issues

- intensiveness — good programs are sustained over time and require active, not passive, involvement by participants
- relevance — good programs are tailored to the needs of the group, place students in leadership roles, and emphasize the relationship of sexual assault to other issues
- positive messages — good programs focus as much on what people can do as on what they should not do, and they reinforce healthy behaviors.

Of the four characteristics cited above, relevance is perhaps the one that is most lacking in programming for men. When we tailor our programming to bring a message that men can view as important to their lives, when we help them understand the social context of sexual assault, and when we empower male students to lead the way in social change, we not only help to reduce the risk of violence, we contribute in a positive way to men's development and the quality of their respectful relationships with women and with one another.

4
Critical Elements of Sexual-Assault Prevention and Risk-Reduction Programs for Men and Women

by Alan D. Berkowitz

Programs to reduce the incidence of sexual assault between acquaintances are common on college and university campuses. Almost all institutions of higher education have educational programs for men and/or women that provide information about the severity and causes of sexual assault and teach participants steps they can take as men and women to prevent it. Yet despite the existence of these programs, there is little consensus in the field regarding what topics and content areas should be covered in workshops for men and/or women.

This chapter is intended to fill this gap. It contains sections on: 1) the characteristics of effective prevention programs, 2) suggested terminology for male and female programs, and; 3) critical program elements that can be incorporated into workshops for men and/or women. Emphasized throughout is the importance of programs tailored to the needs of each gender, whether offered separately or together. While many professionals (including this author) believe that separate gender workshops are preferable, this is not always possible. In either case (separate or coeducational) it is important to acknowledge the different educational needs of women and men and incorporate appropriate material for each gender.

And, regardless of audience format, sexual-assault prevention and risk-reduction programs should incorporate characteristics of effective prevention programs that have been identified in the research and evaluation literature.

The overview of critical program elements provided in the final section of this chapter can also be used as an outline of a comprehensive curriculum for training peer educators and others who provide workshops and programs. Facilitators who are knowledgeable about these issues and comfortable discussing them will be equipped to deal with a wide range of audiences and situations. It may also be helpful to individuals in judicial affairs who hear cases involving sexual assault between acquaintances.

Characteristics of Effective Prevention Programs

The evaluation literature assessing the effectiveness of drug prevention, sexual-assault prevention, and child sexual-abuse prevention programs suggests that effective prevention programs have a number of characteristics which are independent of particular issues or topical areas (Berkowitz 1997; Berkowitz 1998). In particular, effective prevention programs are comprehensive, intensive, relevant to the audience, and deliver positive messages.

Comprehensiveness. Comprehensiveness addresses who is part of the intervention. In a comprehensive program all relevant community members or systems are involved and have clearly defined roles and responsibilities. For example, a workshop for athletes will be more effective if coaches are involved in the planning and are knowledgeable and supportive of the content and purpose of the workshop (Berkowitz 1994a). Linking workshops and lectures provided during orientation and in classes during the year can strengthen the impact of a program. Thus, a scenario on sexual assault or incest presented during a peer theater presentation during orientation can also be discussed and compared to a similar situation read in a novel in a literature class. In general, finding ways to link activities that are normally separate and disconnected can create positive synergy and result in programs that are more effective in combination than alone.

Many prevention specialists have found that offering individual workshops in conjunction with campus media campaigns is an excellent way to provide mutually reinforcing messages. For example, statistics and positive messages reviewed in a workshop can be incorporated into posters and social norms media that are placed around campus to provide a "booster" that strengthens and reinforces the original message.

Achieving comprehensiveness requires that we view the target population as the whole campus community and that we devote time to creating meaningful connections with our colleagues. This will help us be aware of what others are doing, develop a common prevention framework, and provide students with information and messages that are mutually reinforcing, integrated, and synergistic.

Intensiveness. Intensiveness is a function of what happens within a program activity. Programs should offer learning opportunities that are interactive and sustained over time, with active rather than passive participation. In general, interactive interventions are more effective than ones that require only passive participation. For example, interactive theater with audience participation is a more powerful intervention than a presentation without discussion or audience participation. An interactive theater presentation with audience discussion followed by discussion in small groups is an ideal way to combine large and small program formats. Creating intensive programs which foster interaction, discussion and reflection require that we focus on process as well as content, and replace rigid structure with flexibility.

Interactive programs that are sustained over time and that have multiple points of contact with reinforcing messages are stronger than programs that occur at one point in time only. Thus, linking interactive workshops with in-class discussion, as noted above, is more "comprehensive" and "intensive" that a stand-alone program.

Relevance. Programs that are relevant are tailored to the age, community, culture, and socioeconomic status of the recipients and take into consideration an individual's peer-group experience. Creating relevance requires that we acknowledge the special needs and concerns of different communities and affinity groups. Relevance can be accomplished by designing programs for general audiences that are inclusive and acknowledge participant differences, or by designing special programs for particular audiences. Heppner et al. (1999), for example, found that a sexual-assault program that was effective for white men did not have a similar benefit for men of color in the audience. However, when the program was adapted to include material relevant to men of color and was presented by a mixed-race pair, it was found to be effective for all participants in a mixed audience of both white men and men of color. Thus, sexual-assault programs need to have inclusive language and make reference to the different identity groups present on an individual campus. Peer-facilitated programs are considered by many to be desirable because peers can present information and share personal material in a way that is relevant and appropriate to students in a particular campus environment.

Fostering programs that are gender relevant is a goal of this chapter. Since men and women have different needs and socialization experiences, programmatic goals need to be developed that reflect these unique and different needs. A clear consensus is emerging among experts that sexual-assault prevention is most effective when conducted in separate gender groups. For example, the authors of five separate reviews of the evaluation literature on sexual-assault prevention programs have concluded that separate gender programs are the preferred prevention strategy (Brecklin and Forde, in press; Gidycz, Dowdall, and Marioni 2000; Lonsway 1996; Schewe 2000; Yeater and O'Donohue 1999). This conclusion is based on a number of factors, including: the different strategies and goals for men's and women's programs and the danger of inconsistent messages when both groups are combined (Gidycz, Dowdall, and Marioni 2000; Schewe 2000; Yeater and O'Donohue 1999), outcome studies indicating that mixed gender programs are less effective than separate gender programs (Brecklin and Forde, in press; Lonsway 1996), and the testimony of participants in all separate gender workshops (Berkowitz 2000b). Berkowitz (2000b) has provided an extensive discussion of the theory, research, and rationale for working with men separately from women.

Thus, it is recommended here that separate gender programs be conducted when possible. When this is not possible, gender relevant material should be incorporated into coeducational programs so that the different needs of women and men are met to the greatest extent possible.

Relevant programs pay attention to the culture of the problem, the culture of the service or message-delivery system, and the culture of the target population (Berkowitz 2000a). Differences in these three cultures must be addressed in the design of programs. For example, a discussion of sexual assault with an African-American audience should acknowledge the use of rape as a weapon or instrument of slavery. Similarly, men of color may have concerns about judicial and legal systems that are less relevant to a Caucasian audience. Issues such as these should be acknowledged and addressed whenever possible to ensure program inclusiveness and relevance to all participants.

Positive Messages. Positive messages should build on the audiences' values and predisposition to act in a positive manner. Young adults are more receptive to positive messages outlining what can be done rather than negative messages that promote fear or blame. Programs that are blame or induce guilt have been found to have a negative effect on men or even produce a backlash. A good example of an intervention with positive messages has been developed to successfully reduce alcohol consumption on college campuses. This approach, based on social-norms theory, is currently being adapted to the issue of sexual assault (Berkowitz 1998; Berkowitz 2000b). It uses the concept of the "Prevention PIE" to develop messages which are positive, inclusive, and empowering (Haines 1996).

A summary of the characteristics of effective programs is provided in Table 1.

Table 1
Characteristics of Effective Programs*

Comprehensiveness:	Involves all relevant constituencies
	Permeates all aspects of the system
	Targets the community as a whole
	Addresses bystander and enabling issues
Intensiveness:	Activities are sustained over time
	Activities require active (versus passive) involvement
Relevance:	Tailored to the needs of specific groups
	Focus on peer-related variables
	Peers in leadership roles
	Emphasize the relationship of the problem to other issues

*Reprinted with permission from Berkowitz 1997 and Berkowitz 1998.

Table 1 (Continued)
Characteristics of Effective Programs

Positive messages: Healthy behaviors and norms are
                           documented and reinforced

                           Individuals are encouraged to focus
                           on what they can do, not on what
                           they shouldn't do

                           Exclusive emphasis on problem
                           behaviors is avoided

To design a program that incorporates these elements may seem like a daunting task. It is important, therefore, to focus on quality and process rather than quantity. A few interventions that are carefully linked, sequenced, and integrated with other activities in and out of the classroom will be more powerful than many program efforts that are discrete, isolated, and unrelated.

Terminology: Sexual-Assault Prevention, Risk Reduction, Deterrence, and Empowerment

Professionals have struggled to develop adequate terminology to describe men's and women's roles in addressing sexual assault in intimate relationships. An important guideline is that the person who initiates or takes the initiative to increase sexual intimacy is responsible for ensuring that any intimacy is mutual, uncoerced, and consenting. Since sexual activity is typically initiated by men, and because almost all sexual assaults are perpetrated by men against women, children, and/or other men, the term "prevention" in this chapter is primarily used to describe programs directed at male audiences. At the same time, it is important to acknowledge that women can also be perpetrators against children, men, and/or other women, and that women can take steps to prevent assaults from occurring.

Programs for potential victims can help reduce the risk of sexual assault by empowering participants to engage in actions that decrease the likelihood of victimization, although this risk cannot be eliminated. The terms "risk reduction," "deterrence" and "empowerment" are used in this chapter to describe programs which teach women actions that can reduce the potential risk of assault, increase protective factors and skills for self-defense, and foster social activism to end violence against women. Risk-reduction and deterrence strategies can also be considered a form of prevention because they can prevent individuals from becoming victims. Since almost all victims of sexual assaults are women, risk-reduction, safety-enhancement and empowerment programs should primarily be directed at women. However, because a smaller percentage of men may also be victimized, programs with male audiences should acknowledge and be sensitive to issues of male victimization.

All institutions of higher education have the responsibility to devote significant resources to programs that engage men in the task of preventing sexual assault. At the same time, as long as sexual assault remains a reality in women's lives, we have a responsibility to educate and empower women to take steps to reduce the chance of victimization and prevent rape. It is thus not acceptable to focus educational efforts on risk-reduction/deterrence programs for women without an equal or greater focus on men's responsibility for prevention. With this in mind, what are the areas that should be addressed or at least mentioned in programs for men and/or women?

Essential Program Elements

Programs are more effective when the different needs of men and women are addressed. Lack of attention to gender issues has been a major factor in the lack of success of many programs on sexual assault (Lonsway 1996). While there are some program elements or objectives that are shared in common for both genders, there are others that are unique to each. Thus, this section provides an overview of critical program elements or components that are relevant to: 1) both men and women, and 2) program elements which are relevant to only men or only women. It can be used as a checklist to evaluate the comprehensiveness of a program whether it is coeducational, all male, or all female, and with whatever format is used for engaging the audience (i.e., interactive theater, interactive discussion, presentation of a video, etc.). Lists of these program elements are provided below.

Critical Elements of Sexual-Assault Prevention and Risk Reduction Programs

Common Components for Prevention and/or Risk-Reduction Programs

These program elements should be considered for inclusion when women and/or men are in the audience.

1. Emphasize that sexual activity is a choice, and that all people, at any time, are free to choose whether to be sexually active or not.

2. Provide information about the definitions and severity of the problem of sexual assault.

3. Inform participants about relevant campus and/or local laws and policies.

4. Explore characteristics of risky situations.

5. Understand that sexually coercive behavior takes place on a continuum.

6. Address the role of alcohol and other drugs from the perspective of both victim and perpetrator.

7. Distinguish issues of miscommunication from abuse of power or coercion.

8. Educate about heterosexist or ethnic assumptions about sexuality and sex.

9. Understand consent and how to be sure that both parties are fully consenting.

10. Explore relevant aspects of male and female gender socialization and the role of sexism in facilitating sexual assaults.

11. Challenge rape myths and reduce victim blaming.

12. Provide information about campus and community resources and services.

Components of Rape-Prevention Programs for Men

These program elements should be considered for inclusion when men are in the audience in addition to those listed as "Common Components."

1. Emphasize men's responsibility for preventing sexual assault.

2. Understand the range of coercive behaviors that men are socialized to employ.

3. Challenge myths and assumptions regarding the role of sexuality and sexual activity in men's lives.

4. Address men's false fear of false accusation.

5. Reduce enabling and bystander behaviors among men.

6. Increase empathy for victims and understanding of the impact of rape.

7. Acknowledge male victimization.

8. Explore opportunities for men to take social action to raise other men's awareness about the problem of sexual assault.

Components of Risk-Reduction Programs for Women

These program elements should be considered for inclusion when women are in the audience in addition to those listed as "Common Components."

1. Educate women about the characteristics and operational styles of different types of perpetrators.

2. Reduce enabling and bystander behaviors among women that encourage women to take unsafe risks and/or overlook friend's risk-taking.

3. Reduce victim-blaming, increase understanding and support for women who are victimized.

4. Encourage women to access support services specific to the different types of assault.

5. Discuss the effectiveness of different responses to coercive behavior.

6. Understand and overcome cultural norms and socialization experiences that reduce self-efficacy and cause women to overlook internal and external cues about danger.

7. Discuss the different emotional reactions that women may have to assault and emphasize protective behaviors that may reduce vulnerability to assault.

8. Understand risk behaviors that may increase vulnerability to assault and emphasize protective behaviors that may reduce vulnerability to assault

9. Learn self-defense techniques and skills.

10. Explore opportunities for social action to educate about and prevent sexual assault.

It may not be possible to incorporate all of these elements in a particular program, and it may be possible to develop a highly effective program based on only a few. When possible, however, it is important to cover all or most of these at least briefly. A good program encourages active discussion, interaction, and thoughtful integration over content. Thus, the suggested program components should serve as guidelines rather than requirements.

For example, a comprehensive coeducational program would incorporate as many of the objectives in all three categories as possible, while a women's only program would cover the objectives in the "Common" and "Women's" categories. Similarly, a men-only program would cover the objectives in the "Common" and "Men's" categories.

Another use of these program elements is as a training outline for peer educators and staff who will be facilitating programs, or for individuals who will be hearing cases. Familiarity with these issues will ensure that facilitators and hearing board members are exposed to the wide range of issues that are relevant to the issue of sexual assault.

Common Components for Prevention and Risk-Reduction Programs

These program elements should be considered for inclusion when women and/or men are in the audience.

1. *Emphasize that sexual activity is a choice and that all people, at any time, are free to choose whether to be sexually active and how.* In talking about sexual assault, there is a danger of reinforcing the assumption that all or most students are sexually active. In a number of studies cited in Berkowitz (2000a), college students routinely overestimated the amount of sexual activity of their peers, creating increased pressure to be sexually active. It is thus important that the choice to not be sexually active is emphasized and that myths about the presumed sexual activity of college students are debunked.

2. *Provide information about the definitions and severity of the problem of sexual assault.* When possible, this information should be local to your community or campus.

3. *Inform participants about relevant campus and/or local laws and policies. This includes campus policies as well as local and state policies.* When campus jurisdiction for sexual assaults extends off campus, as allowed by the Cleary law, this should be stated. In general, a focus on statistics and information should be minimized to allow time for discussion and interaction. Some students may focus on legal details and definitions as a way of avoiding the interpersonal, moral, and emotional aspects of the issue. Overly legalistic and formalistic discussions should thus be avoided. It is useful to remind participants that if they learn ways to ensure that all sexual intimacy is mutual, uncoerced, and consenting, then concern with the law will become unnecessary.

4. *Explore characteristics of risky situations.* Ambiguity about sexual intent, unresponsiveness on the part of one person (often the female), and unverified assumptions

about what the other person wants are examples of situations that are problematic for both men and women.

5. *Understand that sexually coercive behavior takes place on a continuum.* Participants should be presented with the full range of coercive behaviors, from verbal pressure, implied threats of force, actual force, to rape. *The Sexual Experiences Survey* (Koss and Gidycz 1987) is an excellent survey instrument for documenting the range of coercive behaviors that constitute unwanted intimacy. Presentation of physically violent rapes or situations in which lack of permission is clearly evident, may allow men to disown the possibility that they could also be perpetrators in a more ambiguous situation. Similarly, women may be more prone to engage in self-blame if the possibility of an assault without overt force is not discussed. Thus, the full range of coercive situations, from subtle to overt, and from verbal to physical, should be discussed and represented in examples.

6. *Address the role of alcohol and other drugs from the perspective of both victim and perpetrator (including the use of 'date rape' drugs).* College students report that most sexual intimacy on college campuses takes place after alcohol consumption, and this is true as well for sexual assault. Thus, it is extremely important to discuss the effects of alcohol consumption and the way in which alcohol may be a facilitator of assault. Abbey, Ross, and McDuffie (1994) have identified eight ways in which alcohol may be implicated in a sexual assault perpetrated by a male on a female:

    ♦ It encourages the expression of traditional gender role beliefs about sexual behavior.

- It triggers alcohol expectancies associated with male sexuality and aggression.

- It engages stereotypes about the sexual availability of women who drink alcohol.

- It increases the likelihood that men will misperceive women's friendly cues as a sign of sexual interest.

- It limits women's ability to rectify men's misperceptions of sexual intent.

- It decreases women's capacity to resist sexual assault.

- It is used as justification for men to commit sexual assault.

- It makes women feel responsible for sexual assault.

7. *Distinguish issues of miscommunication from abuse of power or coercion.* Although poor communication is a risk factor for sexual assault, almost all sexual assaults result from one person imposing their wishes on another. Strategies for improving communication assume that both parties have equal power, which is not the case in situations leading to sexual assault. Thus, while communication strategies may be emphasized and can form the basis for a workshop on healthy relationships, they should not be the main focus of sexual-assault prevention/deterrence programs.

8. *Educate about heterosexist or ethnic assumptions about sexuality and sex.* Sexual assault can occur between individuals of any race or sexual orientation. It is thus important to provide information or examples that dispel myths about the identity of perpetrators and victims. One technique for doing this is to provide a scenario that uses names for the perpetrator and victim that could be male

or female (for example, Chris and Pat). A discussion with the audience about their assumptions regarding Chris and Pat's gender and/or race can be illuminating.

9. *Understand consent and how to be sure that both parties are fully consenting.* According to Berkowitz (1994a), consent requires that both parties are fully conscious, have equal ability to act, are positive and sincere in their desires, and have clearly communicated their intent.

10. *Explore relevant aspects of male and female gender socialization and the role of sexism in facilitating sexual assault.* Many of the traditional behaviors and roles that are part of men's and women's socialization can increase the likelihood of sexual assault. These gender roles are taught to all men and women and therefore we are all influenced by them. Educational programs should therefore include discussion of the relationship between gender-role socialization and gender-role stereotyping and sexual assault.

11. *Challenge rape myths and reduce victim blaming.* Myths about victims and perpetrators that serve to justify or condone sexual assault must be discussed and critiqued.

12. *Provide information about campus and community resources and services.*

Components of Rape-Prevention Programs for Men

Men's denial of the problem of sexual assault and the failure of most men to intervene with other men are two main barriers to effective prevention for men. An additional barrier is men's homophobia or fear of closeness with other men. While it may not be practical to address issues of homophobia in a short workshop format, awareness of homophobia is a critical component in the training of facilitators for men's programs so that the issue can be addressed when it surfaces. A discussion of these issues requires a deep understanding of male socialization and culture and the creation of opportunities for men to discuss the discomfort most feel with their socialization as men.

Currently there are a number of programs and curricula focusing on men's responsibility for preventing sexual assault, including workshops by Foubert and his colleagues (Foubert and Marriott 1997; Foubert and McEwen 1998), Mahlstedt and Corcoran (1999), Berkowitz (1994a) and Katz (1995). These programs for men tend to focus on one or more themes: creation of empathy for victims, guidelines for understanding and achieving consent, men's responsibility for confronting other men's inappropriate language and/or behavior, or the relationship of men's socialization to sexual assault. Each of these programs places an emphasis on one or more of the program elements listed below.

1. *Emphasize men's responsibility for preventing sexual assault.* One of the greatest barriers to effective prevention is the assumption on the part of men that sexual assault is a "women's problem." Thus, effective programming for men should clearly outline men's responsibility for prevention and help participants understand how men are hurt by sexual assault, not only indirectly, but directly.

2. *Understand the range of coercive behaviors that men are socialized to employ.* Portrayals of physically violent and/or stranger rapes allow most men (who do not see themselves engaging in such behavior) to distance themselves from the problem. Men must learn that there are more subtle forms of coercion and or influence that operate in interpersonal relationships and take active steps to ensure that equality of choice and action is the basis of

all intimate relationships. In some cases, men may act in a way that is experienced as coercive by another person without realizing that they are acting in this way. Understanding the dynamics of coercive behavior and the possibility of unintentional coercion are critical issues for men.

3. *Challenge myths and assumptions regarding the role of sexuality and sexual activity in men's lives.* Frequent heterosexual sex is equated with masculinity in many men's upbringings, whether or not this is actually true in men's lives. Pressures men feel to be sexually active and to live up to male myths of sexual activity and prowess are thus important to deconstruct and critique.

4. *Address men's false fear of false accusation.* Men's (false) fear of false accusation provides an opportunity to explore strategies for achieving consent and the ways in which men can be unintentionally coercive. While false accusations can occur, they are extremely rare, and their numbers are grossly overestimated by contemporary college men.

5. *Reduce enabling and bystander behaviors among men (for both prevention and postvention).* Programs for men must move beyond a focus on individual responsibility to emphasize men's responsibility to each other to intervene and challenge inappropriate comments, actions, or behavior. Research based on social-norms approaches (Berkowitz 2000a; Kilmartin et al. 1999) have documented that most men are in fact uncomfortable with the behavior of a minority of men who exploit or objectify women. Prevention programs should therefore help men move from passive silence to active opposition and intervention when inappropriate behavior is witnessed.

6. *Increase empathy for victims and understanding the effects of rape.* Most men are capable of empathy and will be inhibited from acting in unintentionally coercive ways when the full effects and trauma of sexual assault are understood. This information can be provided by victim stories and testimony, in skits and vignettes, or by the personal sharing of men who have been secondary victims.

7. *Acknowledge male victimization.* Men may have particular difficulty acknowledging that a boy or man can be the victim of unwanted sex. It is thus important to carefully define and provide statistics on male victimization and explore men's discomfort with discussing this issue.

8. *Explore opportunities for social action to educate about and prevent sexual assault.* For men to truly take on prevention requires a commitment to social activism to end violence against women. Such activism can take many forms, including fund-raising for local rape-crisis centers, political action, participation in Take Back the Night (as appropriate), conducting a White Ribbon Campaign, etc. (Berkowitz, 2000b).

Components of Risk-Reduction, Deterrence, and Empowerment Programs for Women

Naiveté about sexual assault and a false sense of security are two of the greatest risk factors for sexual assault among women. Teaching women steps to reduce the risk of sexual assault and ways to feel a sense of agency and control in the face of threat are critical. The problem is how to accomplish these objectives without promoting victim blame if assaults do occur, and without teaching women to be fearful, threatened, and disempowered.

1. *Educate women about the characteristics and operational styles of different types of perpetrators.* All perpetrators of sexual assault are not the same. Women need the skills and knowledge to identify different types of assaults and styles of perpetration, and to learn warning signs and appropriate responses.

2. *Reduce enabling and bystander behaviors among women that encourage women to take unsafe risks or overlook friends' risk-taking.* Programs for women must go beyond a focus on individual responsibility to emphasize women's responsibility to each other in preventing unintentional enabling or risky behavior.

3. *Reduce victim blaming, increase understanding and support for women who are victimized.* Women are just as likely as men to believe in myths that blame other women for their sexual assaults. These attitudes and beliefs can result in retraumatization of victims and prevent them from accessing counseling, medical, and legal services. Women must therefore be encouraged to identify and critique the attitudes and beliefs that result in victim blaming.

4. *Encourage women to access support services specific to the different types of assault.*

5. *Discuss the effectiveness of different responses to coercive behavior.* A variety of nonverbal, verbal, and physical responses may be effective in response to coercive behavior. Many of these responses are situation specific and can be effectively discussed in reaction to scenarios or role plays. By definition, any increase in the range of behaviors available to women in response to coercive behavior is effective risk reduction or deterrence.

6. *Understand and overcome cultural norms and socialization experiences that reduce self-efficacy and cause women to overlook internal and external cues about danger.* Vulnerability to sexual assault is a direct outcome of how girls are taught to be women. A feminist understanding of women's socialization and experiences is an important component of any work with women.

7. *Discuss the different emotional reactions that women may have to the issue of sexual assault.* Women differ in their understanding of sexual assault and in their emotional responses to it. Creating a safe space for these emotions to surface so that they can be affirmed and discussed is an important goal of programming for women.

8. *Understand risk behaviors that may increase vulnerability to assault and emphasize protective behaviors that may reduce vulnerability to assault.* Women should not be asked to restrict their freedom of action, dress, or behavior in response to the fear of sexual assault. Doing so in effect forces the victim to take responsibility for the behavior of the perpetrator. At the same time, it is prudent for women to understand how certain language, dress, or behavior may be misinterpreted or misunderstood by men so that steps can be taken (out of a sense of power, not fear) to reduce the likelihood of men acting on the basis of these misunderstandings.

9. *Learn self-defense techniques and skills.* Women's empowerment is achieved when women feel able to defend themselves and to use physical force in response to potential or actual assaults. Women who are able to respond forcefully and physically to provocations and attempts at physical coercion can effectively prevent assaults from occurring. The self-esteem inherent in the

ability to defend oneself to whatever extent possible is one of the most effective antidotes to a variety of attitudes and behaviors that may increase women's risk of sexual assault.

Summary and Conclusion

Understanding and eliminating sexual assault requires a sophisticated understanding of how boys are taught to be men and how girls are taught to be women. Sexuality and sexual assault are gendered experiences that are learned. Thus, it is important that sexual-assault programming: 1) acknowledge the different needs, experiences, and perspectives of men and women, and be tailored appropriately, and 2) be designed in a way that is effective and powerful. This chapter has provided an overview of characteristics of effective programs, offered a conceptual definition of programming activities for men and women, and reviewed important elements to be addressed in programs for women and/or men. It is the author's sincere hope that this discussion will advance the "state of the art" in sexual-assault prevention and risk-reduction programs on college and university campuses and promote dialogue in the service of more effective programs.

Appendix A
Resources

Books on Men and Masculinity

Andronico, M. P. (ed.). *Men in Groups: Insights, Interventions, and Psychoeducational Work.* Washington, D.C.: American Psychological Association, 1996.

Brooks, G. R. *The Centerfold Syndrome: How Men Can Overcome Objectification and Achieve Intimacy with Women.* San Francisco: Jossey-Bass, 1995.

Clatterbaugh, K. *Contemporary Perspectives on Masculinity: Men, Women, and Politics in Modern Society,* 2nd ed. Boulder, Colo.: Westview, 1997.

Connell, R. W. *Masculinities.* Berkeley, Calif.: University of California Press, 1995.

Craig, S. (ed.). *Men, Masculinity, and the Media.* Newbury Park, Calif.: Sage, 1992.

Gertner, D. M., and J. E. Harris. *Experiencing Masculinities: Exercises, Activities, and Resources for Teaching and Learning About Men.* Denver: Everyman, 1994.

Gilmore, D. D. *Manhood In the Making: Cultural Concepts of Masculinity.* New Haven, Conn.: Yale University Press, 1990.

Groth, A. N. *Men Who Rape: The Psychology of the Offender.* New York: Plenum, 1979.

Kilmartin, C. T. *The Masculine Self,* 2nd ed. Boston: McGraw-Hill, 2000.

Kimmel, M. S. *Manhood in America: A Cultural History.* New York: Free Press, 1996.

Kimmel, M. S., and M. A. Messner. (eds.). *Men's Lives,* 4th ed. Needham Heights, Mass.: Allyn and Bacon, 1998.

Kupers, T. A. *Revisioning Men's Lives: Gender, Intimacy, and Power.* New York: Guilford, 1993.

Levant, R. F. *Masculinity Reconstructed: Changing the Rules of Manhood — at Work, in Relationships, and in Family Life.* New York: Dutton, 1995.

Levant, R. F., and G. R. Brooks (eds.). *Men and Sex.* New York: Wiley, 1997.

Levant, R. F., and W. S. Pollack (eds.). *A New Psychology of Men.* New York: Basic Books, 1995.

Lynch, J., and C. T. Kilmartin. *The Pain Behind the Mask. Masculine Depression: Causes, Consequences, and Remedies.* Binghamton, N.Y.: Haworth, 1999.

Majors, R., and J. M. Billson. *Cool Pose: The Dilemmas of Black Manhood in America.* New York: Lexington, 1992.

Nardi, P. M. (ed.). *Men's Friendships.* Newbury Park, Calif.: Sage, 1992.

Nelson, J. B. *The Intimate Connection: Male Sexuality, Masculine Spirituality.* Philadelphia: Westminster, 1998.

Pleck, J. H. *The Myth of Masculinity.* Cambridge, Mass.: MIT Press, 1981.

Pollack, W. *Real Boys: Rescuing our Sons From the Myths of Boyhood.* New York: Random House, 1998.

Real, T. *I Don't Want to Talk About It: Overcoming the Secret Legacy of Male Depression.* New York: Scribner, 1997.

Rotundo, E. A. *American Manhood: Transformations in Masculinity From the Revolution to the Modern Era.* New York: Basic Books, 1993.

Sabo, D., and D. F. Gordon. (eds.). *Men's Health and Illness: Gender, Power, and the Body.* Thousand Oaks, Calif.: Sage, 1995.

Zilbergeld, B. *The New Male Sexuality.* New York: Bantam, 1992.

General Books on Gender

Anselmi, D. L., and A. L. Law. (eds.). *Questions of Gender: Perspectives and Paradoxes*. Boston: McGraw-Hill, 1998.

Basow, S. *Gender: Stereotypes and Roles,* 3rd ed. Monterey, Calif.: Brooks/Cole, 1992.

Beall, A. E., and R. J. Sternberg (eds.). *The Psychology of Gender.* New York: Guilford, 1993.

Bem, S. L. *The Lenses of Gender: Transforming the Debate on Sexual Inequality.* New Haven, Conn.: Yale University Press, 1993.

Coontz, S. *The Way We Really Are: Coming to Terms With America's Changing Families.* New York: Basic Books, 1997.

Fausto-Sterling, A. *Myths of gender: Biological Theories About Women and Men,* 3rd ed. New York: Basic Books, 1992.

Johnson, A. G. *The Gender Knot: Unraveling Our Patriarchal Legacy.* Philadelphia: Temple University Press, 1997.

Lerner, G. *The Creation of Patriarchy.* New York: Oxford University Press, 1986.

Lips, H. *Sex and Gender: An Introduction,* 3rd ed. Mountain View, Calif.: Mayfield, 1997.

Rosenblum, K. E., and T. C. Travis, (eds.). *The Meaning of Difference: American Constructions of Race, Sex and Gender, Social Class, and Sexual Orientation.* Boston: McGraw-Hill, 1996.

Books on Sexual Assault and Other Gender-Based Violence

Berkowitz, A. D. (ed.). *Men and Rape: Theory, Research, and Prevention Programs in Higher Education.* San Francisco: Jossey-Bass, 1994.

Blumenfeld, W. J. (ed.). *Homophobia: How We All Pay the Price.* Boston: Beacon, 1992.

Bowker, L. H. (ed.). *Masculinities and Violence.* Thousand Oaks, Calif.: Sage, 1998.

Cromwell, N. A., and A. W. Burgess. (eds.). *Understanding Violence Against Women.* Washington, D.C.: National Academy Press, 1996.

Earle, J. P. "Acquaintance Rape Workshops: Their Effectiveness in Changing the Attitudes of First-Year College Men." Unpublished doctoral dissertation, University of Connecticut, 1992.

Funk, R. E. *Stopping Rape: A Challenge for Men.* Philadelphia: New Society, 1993.

Kivel, P. *Men's Work: How to Stop the Violence that Tears our Lives Apart.* Center City, Minn.: Hazleden, 1992.

Koss, M. P., L. A. Goodman, A. Browne, L. F. Fitzgerald, G. Puryear Keita, and N. Felipe Russo. *No Safe Haven: Male Violence Against Women at Home, at Work, and in the Community.* Washington, D.C.: American Psychological Association, 1994.

Mahlstedt, D. *Getting Started: A Dating Violence Peer-Education Program for Men.* West Chester, Penn.: self-published, 1998.

Miedzian, M. *Boys Will Be Boys: Breaking the Link Between Masculinity and Violence.* New York: Doubleday, 1991.

Parrot, A., N. Cummings, and T. Marchell. *Rape 101: Sexual Assault Prevention for College Athletes*. Holmes Beach, Fla.: Learning Publications, 1994.

Parrot, A., and L. Bechofer (eds.). *Acquaintance Rape: The Hidden Crime*. New York: Wiley, 1991.

Pharr, S. *Homophobia: A Weapon of Sexism*, (expanded edition). Little Rock, Ark.: Chardon, 1997.

Russell, D. E. H. *Dangerous Relationships: Pornography, Misogyny, and Rape*. Thousand Oaks, Calif.: Sage, 1998.

Sanday, P. R. *Fraternity Gang Rape: Sex, Brotherhood, and Privilege on Campus*. New York: New York University Press, 1990.

Sanday, P. R. *A Woman Scorned: Acquaintance Rape on Trial*. New York: Doubleday, 1996.

Scarce, M. *Male on Male Rape: The Hidden Toll of Stigma and Shame*. New York: Plenum, 1997.

Schwartz, M. D., and W. S. DeKeseredy. *Sexual Assault on the College Campus: The Role of Male Peer Support*. Thousand Oaks, Calif.: Sage, 1997.

Toch, H. *Violent Men: An Inquiry Into the Psychology of Violence*. Washington, D.C.: American Psychological Association, 1992.

Organizations

Men's Rape Prevention Project
P.O. Box 57144
Washington, DC 20037-7144
(202) 265-6530
info@mrpp.org
www.mrpp.org

Mentors in Violence Prevention (MVP)
Northeastern University's Center for the Study
of Sport in Society
360 Huntington Avenue, Suite 161 CP
Boston, MA 02115
Phone: (617) 373-4025
http://www.sportinsociety.org/cssswwwPages/cssspage/mvp.html

The White Ribbon Campaign
365 Bloor St. East, Suite 1600
Toronto, Ontario, Canada M4W 3L4
(416) 920-6684
(800) 328-2228
whiterib@idirect.com
www.whiteribbon.ca

Fraternity Violence Education Project
Dr. Deborah Mahlstedt
Dept. of Psychology
West Chester University
West Chester, PA
610-436-3523
dmahlstedt@wcupa.edu
www.wcupa.edu (university website)

National Organization for Men Against Sexism (NOMAS)
P.O. Box 509
Oswego, NY 13827
(607) 697-6179
www.nomas.org

Men Stopping Rape
306 N. Brooks St.
Madison, WI 53715
(608) 257-4444
msr@danenet.wicip.orgdanenet.wicip.org/msr

Appendix B
Outline

I.   Gender is a set of cultural forces that pressure people to experience themselves and to behave in certain ways based on whether they are male or female.

    A.   People tend to think of males and females as different, but research indicates that the sexes are overwhelmingly more similar than different. The diversity within women as a group and within men as a group is greater by far than the small differences we see between the *average* behaviors of males and females.

    B.   People tend to talk about the "opposite sex" and the "battle of the sexes" despite the facts that the sexes are not opposite at all (reproductive roles are complementary, not opposite) and the overwhelming majority of "combatants" in the "battle" are allegedly in love with and having children with the "enemy." Speaking of men and women as opposites is like describing an Apple computer as the opposite of an IBM.

    C.   Gender roles may have a small component of biological influence, but they are mainly learned.

    D.   Gender is a set of social pressures to behave in certain ways, however the responses of individual men and women to these pressures are highly variable — we all know very emotional men or very ambitious women, men who don't like sports or women who do.

        1.   Gender has unconscious and emotional components. People are not always aware of the effects of gender on their lives. These pressures operate like the default options on a computer — it is dif-

ficult to make informed choices about options unless you know that these options exist.

2. Some people conform very strongly to gender
    role stereotypes; some reject these images com-
    pletely; most people fall somewhere in between.

3. Most people behave more gender stereotypically
    in public than in private, indicating that a signifi-
    cant component of gendered behavior is in the
    fulfillment of a social role, rather than merely the
    expression of ingrained characteristics.

4. In every case, people have choices about the ex-
    tent to which they will conform to gender pres-
    sures, and regardless of these pressures, people
    are responsible for the choices that they make.

E. Gender ideologies affect what we expect of people,
    what we notice about them, what we remember about
    them, and how we interact with them. Mainstream U.S.
    culture often puts gender into places where it does not
    belong, such as in color preferences, personality traits,
    types of drinks, how one should sit or carry books, etc.

F. Historically, gender roles seem to be constructed
    around the work that a society needs to do. Gender
    roles are changing because the character of work is
    changing, due to the economic base of society, labor
    saving devices, and reproductive technologies and
    needs.

G. There is some cultural variation to standards of mascu-
    linity within the United States and the world, but there
    is a great deal of overlap in masculine ideologies
    among different cultural groups.

H. Gender roles will continue to evolve in the future, and holding on to 1950s ideas of the social places of men and women will become increasingly untenable.

II. Cultural masculinity is a set of gender pressures placed on males.

    A. Central to the masculine gender role is *antifemininity* — men are expected to avoid culturally defined feminine behaviors at all costs.

    B. Thus, men are expected to constantly prove a negative, which is impossible.

    C. Men who accept masculine ideologies try to avoid:

        1. Vulnerable emotions (most feelings except for anger and lust).

        2. Dependence on others.

        3. Relationship orientation.

        4. Physical safety concerns.

        5. Doing what they believe to be "women's work," such as child care.

        6. Asking for help.

        7. Getting emotionally close to other men.

        8. Exhibiting feminine mannerisms.

        9. Engaging in feminine activities.

    D. The "rules" of masculinity are:

        1. "No sissy stuff" — Avoid feminine behaviors.

        2. "Be a big wheel" — Strive for status and achievement, especially in sports and work.

        3. "Be a male machine" — Solve problems without help, maintain emotional self-control at all times, and never show weakness to anybody.

       4.   "Give 'em hell" — Take physical risks and be violent if necessary.

  E.   Antifemininity is used to enforce conformity to masculine behavior norms. Males can be socially ostracized or even attacked if they behave in feminine ways. One of the worst insults that one can level on a boy is that he throws, runs, talks, or acts like a girl.

       1.   Antifemininity encourages men to see themselves as having nothing in common with women. This inhibits the formation of friendships with women and equal-partner types of romantic relationships with women. Despite the cultural pressure of the antifemininity norm, many men are able to achieve these kinds of relationships with women.

       2.   Antifemininity also inhibits men from learning from women. Many culturally defined feminine traits and skills (e.g., emotional expression, relationship sensitivity, self-protection) have important implications for people's quality of life, yet many men avoid taking on these traits and learning these skills because they fear being considered unmasculine.

  F.   One of the most feminine kinds of behavior is getting too close to another man. Masculinity tends to sexualize all intimacy. *Homophobia*, the fear of same sex attraction, is related to antifemininity and is also used to enforce gender conformity in men. Another worst insult to level at a male is to suggest that he is sexually attracted to other males.

III. Conformity to masculine ideologies has both advantages and disadvantages:

A. Advantages:

1. A fairly clear "road map" for behavior and a convenient "yardstick" for measuring one's worth.

2. Approval and admiration of others in many situations.

3. A sense of power if one is "successful".

4. Achievement and problem-solving that contributes to the greater good.

5. Infrequent and/or less intense experience of negative emotions.

6. A high likelihood that others will take one seriously.

B. Disadvantages:

1. Must always compete and achieve.

2. Can never prove a negative.

3. Infrequent and/or less intense experience of positive emotions.

4. physical health problems. Men:

    a. die an average of seven years earlier than women.

    b. commit suicide four times more often.

    c. are at greater risk for most serious diseases.

    d. are injured more often.

    e. the acceptance of hypermasculine ideologies is related to a number of health risks.

5. Mental health problems. Men:

    a. abuse alcohol and other drugs more frequently.

   b. are hospitalized in psychiatric facilities fol-
    lowing a relationship breakup much more
    frequently than women.

   c. receive little social support if they are stereo-
    typically masculine.

  6. Loneliness: Hypermasculine men have many
   "buddies," but few true friends. If they are heterosexual, their relationships with women are
   often impoverished because of their need to be
   distant from the feminine.

  7. Violence: Males commit over 90 percent of violent crimes, and there are currently more than one
   million men in federal prisons.

IV. Social advantages and disadvantages are gender-based to an
 extent.

  A. To be male in U.S. culture is to have a set of social advantages, such as the freedom to express one's sexual
   needs, occupational opportunity, and lower fear of gender-based violence relative to women.

   1. These advantages do not apply to all men in equal
    shares. Wealthy, white, attractive, heterosexual,
    able-bodied, and athletic men tend to reap more
    advantages than other men.

   2. There are social disadvantages to the advantages
    of being male, such as paying full price for drinks
    at "ladies nights," being judged by one's athletic
    and business accomplishments, and having others
    pay little attention to our physical or emotional
    pain.

  B. To be female in U.S. culture is to have a set of social
   disadvantages, such as lower pay than males for the

same work, being judged by one's attractiveness, and disproportionate exposure to sexual harassment, sexual assault, and other forms of gender-based violence.

1. These disadvantages do not apply to all women in equal shares. Wealthy, white, attractive, heterosexual, and able-bodied women tend to reap fewer disadvantages than other women.

2. There are social advantages to the disadvantages of being female, such as paying less than full price for drinks at "ladies nights," getting a good deal of attention if one is attractive, and sometimes having others pay attention to one's physical or emotional pain.

C. Social advantages and disadvantages are best viewed in relative terms and multiple contexts. One cannot consider a person privileged merely because that person enjoys some isolated advantage. For example, a "big picture" analysis would never consider the following people privileged:

1. Handicapped people because they get good parking places.

2. People in prison because they don't have to pay for their meals.

3. People in menial jobs because they don't have to take their work home with them.

D. Likewise, one cannot consider a person underprivileged merely because that person suffers some isolated disadvantage. For example, a "big picture" analysis would never consider the following people underprivileged:

1. People who can afford to hire maids and servants because it compromises their privacy.

2. Famous people because their fans want to talk with them when they go out in public.

3. Strikingly attractive people because they get so much attention from people who want to date them.

V. Traditional masculinity and traditional femininity are becoming outmoded because:

A. Reproductive technologies and overpopulation mean that couples can decide when, and if they will have children and decide how many they will have. Except for breastfeeding, men can perform every parenting behavior. Therefore, reproductive roles are much more flexible than ever.

B. Upper body strength is no longer an important economic asset, as labor-saving devices are now available for most tasks.

C. We are moving from an industrial to an information-based economy, and therefore people can even work at home.

D. Because of these changes, women are becoming equal economic partners, and therefore "breadwinning" no longer exclusively defines masculinity, and homemaking no longer exclusively defines femininity. Heterosexual couples have a greater amount of options in negotiating their work and family roles.

VI. Most college men:

A. Want to have a successful college career and graduate.

B. Want to enter the working world, do well, and be financially successful.

C. See themselves in leadership positions in their careers.

D. Will be working with women.

E. May have female supervisors at some points during their working lives.

F. Want to have good relationships with co-workers, subordinates, and supervisors.

G. If heterosexual, want to someday marry, have children, and have satisfying family relationships.

VII. Gender awareness will serve men in all of these goals. Men can expand their notions of masculinity by doing the following:

A. Independence is masculine. Men can be independent by refusing to conform to stereotypical gender demands when they think it is important to do so.

B. Facing a challenge is masculine. Men can face challenges by learning skills that are adaptive but that also have been defined as feminine:

1. dealing with vulnerable emotions,

2. gaining relationship skills,

3. expanding their interests beyond work and sports,

4. learning how to confront male peers who behave in sexist and/or self-destructive ways.

C. Leadership is masculine. Men can be leaders by showing other people a healthier and more modern vision of masculinity.

D. Risk taking is masculine. Men can take reasonable emotional risks by revealing themselves to others in the service of building relationships.

E. Courage is masculine. It takes a good deal of courage to negotiate one's life without using the stereotypical road map of masculinity. It takes great courage to challenge other men who behave in offensive or unhealthy ways.

F. Assertiveness is masculine. Men can be assertive by exercising their rights to express their feelings, questioning outmoded notions of masculinity, and asking for what they want in relationships.

VIII. Many men have distorted notions of the meaning of masculine attributes:

A. *Courage* is facing risk because a successful outcome is important to one's principles and goals. Many men narrowly define risk as only physical or financial, but risk can be emotional or relationship-oriented. *Bravado* is pretended courage — facing risk in order to avoid being evaluated as weak, such as when a man engages in a fight with a bigger opponent because he does not want to be considered unmasculine.

B. *Loyalty* is being faithful to others to whom one has made a commitment. With male friends, many men confuse loyalty with the notion that "anything my friend does is all right with me." It is very disloyal to witness a friend doing something destructive to himself or others and not challenging him. It is disloyal to one's female friends, relatives, and partner to condone or encourage male friends' sexist behaviors and attitudes.

C. *Independence* is freedom of action. It means that one makes up one's own mind about behavior and attitudes rather than blindly conforming to others' opinions. *Counterdependence* or *oppositionalism* is behaving in contrary ways merely to avoid the appearance of being dominated by another person, such as when a man treats his female partner badly in the company of his male friends in order to gain their approval. Although men think of themselves as independent, there is tremendous conformity to masculine ideologies, behaviors, and attitudes in all-male social groups.

D. *Respect* is courteous regard, attention, and consideration for others' feelings and experiences. Stereotypical *chivalry* is a set of rigid rules for men's behavior when in the company of women, such as opening doors for them, ordering their food in a restaurant, or defending them.

   1. Some women view stereotypical chivalric behavior as offensive — they feel that it infantalizes them. Therefore, it is disrespectful to engage in these behaviors in the company of such a person.

   2. Respect is only achieved through careful attention to another person's needs and experiences. It cannot be achieved simply through the application of a rigid set of rules.

IX. All people want respect in their relationships with others. All relationships between two people work best when the partnership has achieved high levels of mutual respect. Fully respectful relationships have the following characteristics:

A. Each partner has equal influence over the activities of the partnership.

B. Both people are equally free to speak without interruption and with the full attention of the other. Partners negotiate conflicts by asking for what they want and being willing to listen and compromise.

C. Each person expresses positive regard for the other both in direct contact and in the company of people outside the dyad. Extremes of disrespect involve name calling, insults, or the use of infantalizing terms such as referring to an adult female as a girl.

D. Each person keeps private that information that he/she has agreed to keep in confidence.

E. Both people engage in constructive and respectful criticism of the other's behavior.

F. Partners can disagree with each other.

G. Both people can comfortably spend time away from each other and in different kinds of relationships.

H. Each partner respects the other's personal boundaries and expresses affection toward the other only with full consent, which has the following characteristics:

   1. Both people are fully conscious.

   2. Each partner is equally free to act.

   3. Both partners are sincere and positive in their desires.

   4. Both partners have clearly communicated their intent.

X. Respect-disrespect is a continuum with full respect at one pole and violence, the ultimate disrespect, on the other.

   A. Somewhere on the continuum, disrespectful behaviors cross the line into illegal acts.

B. Colleges and universities have policies regarding the disrespect of others, especially around sexual assault and sexual harassment, that also draw a line between what is allowed and what is unacceptable.

C. However, people should strive for fully respectful relationships, not mere compliance with law and/or campus policy.

D. Sexual assault and harassment are significant problems on college campuses and elsewhere, and perpetrators are overwhelmingly male.

E. Most sexual assault perpetrators are men who know their victims.

F. In most of these acquaintance rapes, perpetrator and/or victim have been drinking alcohol. However, alcohol is not the cause of the assault. Many men drink and yet would never commit a sexual assault. Some perpetrators try to get their victims drunk and isolate them from others so that they can attack.

G. Despite beliefs to the contrary, most sexual assaults are not the result of misunderstandings between two people; they are predatory and usually planned attacks on the part of the perpetrator.

H. Despite beliefs to the contrary, sexual assault is not the result of a failure of control over one's sexual feelings. Rather it is an act of violence. In a consensual sexual encounter, a man would stop if the couple were interrupted by others, especially the woman's parents. Therefore, men are capable of controlling their behavior even in a state of high sexual arousal.

I. Although all men are not potential perpetrators, these behaviors are related to the culture of masculinity, and therefore solutions can be found in understanding and changing the negative aspects of this culture. Men have an important role to play in reducing all forms of disrespect toward women, and it is a role that goes beyond merely refraining from disrespectful behaviors.

XI.   In order for a sexual assault to take place, at least three conditions must be present:

A.   Individual pathology on the part of the perpetrator: research indicates that perpetrators differ from normal, healthy men in a number of ways, for example:

1.   Extreme acceptance of hypermasculine ideologies.

2.   High levels of hostility toward women.

3.   Feelings that they could not be "man enough" to suit their fathers.

4.   Belief in "rape myths" — that "no" sometimes means "maybe" or "yes", and that women like to be forced into having sex.

5.   ˙Adversarial sexual beliefs — that men and women are enemies and that a date is a kind of competition in which the man tries to get sex and the woman tries to get affection and/or get the man to spend money on her.

6.   Feelings of having been harmed or ridiculed by women.

7.   An experience of physical, emotional, and/or sexual abuse as children, which they have not dealt with in any direct way.

8. A tendency to externalize their own emotional pain and have little empathy for the pain of others.

B. A decision on the part of the perpetrator: regardless of individual pathology, a perpetrator makes a choice to engage in violent behavior, and he is responsible for his choice.

C. Cultural/social support: sexual assault takes place in a social context in which men are encouraged to:

1. See themselves as different from and better than women.

2. Feel entitled to sex and other pleasures by virtue of their status as men.

3. View women as sexual objects whose feelings are not worthy of consideration.

4. Attain status among their male friends by being detached from women and having sex with many different women.

5. Be ready for sex at all times.

6. Overpower women by going after what they want and never taking "no" for an answer.

7. Prove that one is not gay by having sex with women.

8. See sex as set of tasks and techniques rather than a relational behavior between two people.

9. Convert all emotional experiences into anger and/or lust. Vulnerable feelings are seen as completely in control; anger and lust as being completely out of control.

10. View sexual feelings as taking place only in the penis.

11. View violence as an acceptable way to solve problems.

XII. Most men never commit sexual assault because:

A. They respect women.

B. They do not want to hurt another human being.

C. They are not violent.

D. They want relationships with women that are based on love and affection.

E. They fear being punished or lack sexual opportunities.

XIII. All men can help to reduce sexual assault by:

A. Engaging in sexual behavior only with mutual, uncoerced consent.

B. Striving for fully respectful relationships.

C. Modeling respect for women to other men.

D. Refusing to participate in cultural events that support a view of violence as masculine, such as "professional wrestling", action/adventure movies, and violent television or music.

E. Refusing to participate in activities that denigrate women, such as:

1. Use of pornography, especially violent pornography.

2. Sexual objectification, such as rating women's bodies in public, patronizing stripper bars or restaurants like "Hooters," and talking with male friends about women solely in sexual terms.

3. Exhibiting negative attitudes toward women in sexist humor or using terms that animalize ("bitch," "fox"), dehumanize ("whore," "slut") or infantalize ("girl," "baby") women.

4. Laughing or giving other approval when other men behave in sexist ways.

5. Challenging other men's masculinity by using antifemininity ("take off your skirt and play like a man"), homophobia ("only a fag wouldn't have another shot of liquor") or masculine shame ("what are you, a wus?").

6. Bragging about sexual conquest or approving of other men who brag.

F. Refusing to condone dangerous attitudes by being a passive bystander when male friends behave in sexist ways, even when no women are present. To challenge male friends who behave in such ways, a man must:

1. Notice the sexist behavior.

2. See the behavior as a problem that affects one personally.

3. Take responsibility for doing something about it.

4. Have the skills to intervene.

G. Learning about gender and masculinity, and making conscious choices about one's behaviors rather than blindly conforming to gender stereotypes.

H. Embracing gender-based violence as a "men's issue".

I. Becoming a peer educator.

J. Participating in consciousness raising and social change efforts to decrease men's gender-based violence.

XIV. Summary

    A. Men receive a great deal of social pressure to behave in hypermasculine ways, yet most men are kind and sensitive people who do not fit the cultural stereotype.

    B. Most men overestimate the degree to which other men are comfortable with sexism and other hypermasculine behavior, because they compare their inner reactions to other men's appearances. Therefore, they do not often challenge other men's attitudes because they feel that they are different.

    C. Understanding these gender forces frees men to discover who they truly are and make affirmative choices about their behaviors and attitudes rather than conforming to culturally-based gender stereotypes.

    D. Situational factors that empower men to break conformity:

        1. The perception that one has at least one ally in the social group.

        2. An understanding that the bystander role is not neutral.

        3. An awareness that hypermasculinity and sexism are toxic.

        4. An acceptance of responsibility for one's peers.

        5. The presence of appropriate models of alternatives to hypermasculine behaviors.

        6. The principle of commitment: while we look to our attitudes to shape our behaviors, we also look to our behaviors to shape our attitudes. Therefore, taking a behavioral course of action strengthens the attitude. Challenging a hypermasculine behav-

ior makes it more likely that one will think it important to do so.

7.   Having the skills to intervene.

E.   The rewards of becoming gender aware are:

1.   More freedom of choice about one's goals, behaviors, and attitudes.

2.   Fewer physical and mental health problems and risks.

3.   More rewarding relationships of all kinds.

4.   A fuller emotional life.

5.   Increased opportunities for success in all areas of one's life.

Appendix C
References

Abbey, A., L. Thomson Ross, and D. McDuffie. "Alcohol's Role in Sexual Assault." In R. R. Watson (ed.), *Drug and Alcohol Abuse Reviews: Addictive Behaviors in Women.* Totowa, N.Y.: Humana Press 5 (1993): 97-123.

Aronson, E.. "The Power of Self Persuasion," *American Psychologist* 54 (1999): 875-84.

Asch, S. E. "Effects of Group Pressure Upon the Modification and Distortion of Judgments." In H. Proshansky and B. Seidenberg (eds.), *Basic Studies in Social Psychology.* New York: Holt, Rinehart, and Winston, 1965.

Berkowitz, A. D. "A Model Acquaintance Rape Prevention Program for Men." In A. Berkowitz (ed.), *Men and Rape: Theory, Research, and Prevention Programs in Higher Education.* San Francisco: Jossey-Bass, 1994a, pp. 35-42.

Berkowitz, A. D. "The Role of Coaches in Rape Prevention Programs for Athletes. In A. Parrot, N. Cummings, and T. Marchell (eds). *Rape 101: Sexual Assault Prevention for College Athletes.* Holmes Beach, Fla.: Learning Publications, 1994b, pp. 61-64.

Berkowitz, A. D. "From Reactive to Proactive Prevention: Promoting an Ecology of Health on Campus." In P. C. Rivers and E. Shore (eds*.), A Handbook on Substance Abuse for College and University Personnel.* Westport, Conn.: Greenwood, 1997, pp. 119-39.

Berkowitz, A. D. "How We Can Prevent Sexual Harassment and Sexual Assault," *Educators Guide to Controlling Sexual Harassment* 6/1 (1998): 1-4.

Berkowitz, A. D.. "Where Have We Come From and Where Are We Going?" Paper presented at the 9th International Conference on Sexual Assault and Harassment on Campus, Orlando, Fla., 1999.

Berkowitz, A. D. "Applications of Social Norms Theory to Other Health and Social Justice Issues." In H. W. Perkins (ed). *The Social Norms Approach to Prevention,* under review 2000a.

Berkowitz, A. D. "Fostering Men's Responsibility for Preventing Sexual Assault." In P. A. Schewe, (ed.) *Preventing Intimate Partner Violence: Developmentally Appropriate Interventions Across the Lifespan.* Washington D.C.: American Psychological Association, in press 2000b.

Berkowitz, A. D., M. Haines, K. Johannessen, and J. Linkenbach. "Selected How-to's, Do's, and Don't's, and Lessons for Implementing Social Norms Media Campaigns," *Health Education Section Newsletter,* American College Health Association (Fall 1998).

Boswell, A. A., and J. Z. Spade. "Fraternities and Collegiate Rape Culture: Why Are Some Fraternities More Dangerous Places for Women?" *Gender and Society* 10/2 (1996): 133-47.

Brecklin, L. R., and D. R. Forde. *Evaluating the Effectiveness of Rape Intervention Programs: A Meta-Analysis.* Manuscript submitted for publication, University of Illinois.

Brannon, R. "Dimensions of the Male Sex Role in America." In A.G. Sargent, *Beyond Sex Roles,* 2nd ed. New York: West, 1985, pp. 296-316.

Coltrane, S. "Theorizing Masculinities in Contemporary Social Science." In D. L. Anselmi and A. L. Law (eds.), *Questions of gender: Perspectives and Paradoxes.* Boston: McGraw-Hill, 1998, pp. 76-88.

Corcoran, C. B. "From Victim Control to Social Change: A Feminist Perspective on Campus Rape Prevention Programs." In J.

Chrisler and D. Howard (eds.), *New Directions in Feminist Psychology*. New York: Springer, 1992, pp. 130-40.

Earle, J. P. "Acquaintance Rape Workshops: Their Effectiveness in Changing the Attitudes of First-Year College Men." Unpublished doctoral dissertation, University of Connecticut, 1992.

Foubert, J. D., and K. A. Marriott. "Effects of a Sexual Assault Peer Education Program on Men's Beliefs in Rape Myths," *Sex Roles* 36/3-4 (1997): 259-68.

Foubert, J. D., and M. K. McEwen. "An All-Male Rape Prevention Peer Education Program: Decreasing Fraternity Men's Behavioral Intent to Rape," *Journal of College Student Development* 39/6 (1998): 548-56.

Gidycz, C. A, C. L. Dowdall, and N. L. Marioni. "Interventions to Prevent Rape and Sexual Assault." In J. Petrak and B. Hedge (eds.) *The Trauma of Adult Sexual Assault: Treatment, Prevention, and Policy*. New York: Wiley, in press.

Gilmore, D. D. *Manhood in the Making: Cultural Concepts of Masculinity*. New Haven, Conn.: Yale University Press, 1990.

Groth, A. N. *Men Who Rape: The Psychology of the Offender*. New York: Plenum, 1979.

Haines, M. *A Social Norms Approach to Preventing Binge Drinking at Colleges and Universities*. Newton, Mass.: U.S. Department of Education, 1997.

Haney, C., C. Banks, P. and Zimbardo. "Interpersonal Dynamics in a Simulated Prison," *International Journal of Criminology and Penology* 1 (1973): 69-97.

Heppner, M. J., H. A. Neville, K. S. Smith, D. M. Kivlighan, and B. S. Gershuny. "Examining Immediate and Long-Term Efficacy of Rape Prevention Programming with Racially Diverse College Men," *Journal of Counseling Psychology* 46/1 (1999): 16-26.

Hyde, J. S., and E. A. Plant. "Magnitude of Psychological Gender Differences: Another Side to the Story," *American Psychologist* 50 (1995): 159-61.

Katz, J. "Reconstructing Masculinity in the Locker Room: The Mentors in Violence Prevention Project," *Harvard Educational Review*, 65/2 (1995): 163-74.

Koss, M. P., and C. A. Gidycz. "Sexual Experiences Survey: Reliability and Validity," *Journal of Consulting and Clinical Psychology* 55 (1987): 162-70.

Kilmartin, C. T. *The Masculine Self,* 2nd ed. Boston: McGraw-Hill, 2000.

Kilmartin, C. T., B. Chirico, and M. Leemann. "The White Ribbon Campaign: Evidence for Social Change on a College Campus." Paper presented at the Spring Convention of the Virginia Psychological Association, 1997.

Kilmartin, C. T., A. Conway, A. Friedberg, T. McQuoid, T. Tschan, and T. Norbet. "Using the Social Norms Model to Encourage Male College Students to Challenge Rape-supportive Attitudes in Male Peers." Paper presented at the Virginia Psychological Association Spring Conference, Virginia Beach, Va., April 1999.

Lisak, D. "Male Gender Socialization and the Perpetration of Sexual Abuse." In R. F. Levant and G. R. Brooks (eds.), *Men and Sex.* New York: Wiley, 1997, pp. 156-77.

Lisak, D., and Roth, S. "Motivational Factors in Nonincarcerated Sexually Aggressive Men." *Journal of Personality and Social Psychology* 55 (1988): 795-802.

Lonsway, K. A. "Preventing Acquaintance Rape Through Education: What Do We Know?" *Psychology of Women Quarterly* 20 (1996): 229-65.

Mahlstedt, D. *Getting Started: A Dating Violence Peer Education Program for Men.* West Chester, Penn.: self-published, 1998.

Mahlstedt, D., and C. Corcoran. "Preventing Dating Violence." In C. Crawford, S. David, and J. Sebrechts, (eds), *Coming Into Her Own.* San Francisco: Jossey Bass, 1999, pp. 311-27.

Mayer, F. S., S. Duval, and V. H. Duval. "An Attributional Analysis of Commitment," *Journal of Personality and Social Psychology* 39 (1980): 1072-080.

Milgram, S. "Behavioral Study of Obedience," *Journal of Abnormal and Social Psychology* 67 (1963): 371-78.

Rosenthal, R. *Pygmalion in the Classroom.* New York: Irvington, 1996.

Sanday, P. R. "The Socio-Cultural Context of Rape: A Cross-Cultural Study," *Journal of Social Issues* 37 (1981): 5-27.

Schewe, P. A. "Guidelines for Developing Rape Prevention and Risk Reduction Interventions for Adolescents and Young Adults: Lessons From Evaluation Research." In P. A. Schewe, (ed.), *Preventing Intimate Partner Violence: Developmentally Appropriate Interventions Across the Lifespan.* Washington D.C.: American Psychological Association, in press.

Sluser, R., and M. Kaufman. "The White Ribbon Campaign: Mobilizing Men to Take Action." Paper presented at the 17th National Conference on Men and Masculinity, Chicago, Ill., July 1992.

Tavris, C., and C. Wade. *Psychology in Perspective,* 3rd ed. New York: Longman, 2000.

Yeater, E. A., and W. O. O'Donohue. "Sexual Assault Prevention Programs: Current Issues, Future Directions, and the Potential Efficacy of Interventions with Women," *Clinical Psychology Review* 19/7 (1999): 739-71.

About the Authors

Dr. Christopher Kilmartin is an Associate Professor of Psychology at Mary Washington College in Fredericksburg, Va. He holds a Ph.D. in Counseling Psychology from Virginia Commonwealth University.

Dr. Kilmartin is an author, consultant, psychotherapist, teacher, playwright, and performer with expertise in the areas of men's issues, diversity, and violence prevention. He is a licensed clinical psychologist who has a great deal of experience consulting with businesses, college students, human services workers, and counselors. He has also been involved in national leadership of the White Ribbon Campaign, a grass-roots effort to decrease men's violence against women.

His major scholarly work is *The Masculine Self*, 2nd ed., (McGraw-Hill 2000), a psychology of men textbook. He is co-author (with Dr. John Lynch) of *The Pain Behind the Mask: Overcoming Masculine Depression* (Haworth 1999). Dr. Kilmartin is also a professional standup comedian who has written a solo performance theatre piece on men's issues entitled *Crimes Against Nature*. This work, an integration of his scholarly and performing interests, and performed by the author, debuted in 1998 and has toured to over 60 college campuses and 25 other venues across the United States. Dr. Kilmartin can be reached at 540-654-1562 or ckilmart@mwc.edu.

Dr. Alan Berkowitz holds a Ph.D. in Psychology from Cornell University. He is an independent consultant who works with colleges, universities, public-health agencies and communities to create programs that improve health and promote social justice. He is highly regarded for his research, innovative programming, and public speaking, developed one of the first rape-prevention programs for men, and is a central figure in the development and implementation of Social Norms Theory. Alan can be reached at 607-387-3789 or at alan@fltg.net.